'Dr. Robbins offers a remarkable psychoanalytic theory of the structures of mind replacing Freud's tripartite model that incorporates findings from evolutionary biology and primatology. While mankind shares a primordial mind with other animals, the difference is the acquisition of reflection, an ability put on the map by John Locke. It is the ability to speak and to reflect that creates the power to heal.'

Henry Lothane, clinical professor of Psychiatry Icahn
School of Medicine

'Distinguishing the different roles of primordial consciousness and abstract representational thought, this book highlights the limitations of Freud's model of mental structures and conscious and unconscious mind and proposes a different model. Robbins explores the origins of the capacity to reflect on one's mind that distinguishes humans from other species. This book is an intellectual tour de force that integrates psychology and psychoanalysis with neurobiology, linguistic and other sciences: a must read for psychoanalysts and for all readers interested in the deepest dimensions of "homo sapiens".'

Riccardo Lombardi, MD, author of
Body-Mind Dissociation and *Formless Infinity*

WHAT MAKES HUMANS UNIQUE

Through an integrated multi-disciplinary theory, Michael Robbins proposes that the human mind consists of two mental structures: the one we share with other animate creatures and a capacity for reflective representational thought which is unique.

As an alternative to Freud's model of the human mind as structured by the id, ego, and superego, this book contends that the prolonged period of post-natal immaturity – otherwise known as neoteny – which is specific to humans, gives rise to reflective representational thought that in turn allows for the acquisition of complex knowledge. Robbins examines how Freud's conception of the human mind was limited by his ignorance of the related disciplines of sociology, primatology, cultural anthropology, and most notably evolution, which were then in their infancy, to explore the implications of the non-unitary nature of the human mind for us as individuals, as a society, and for our future as a species.

Drawing on a broad range of influences from psychoanalysis to anthropology, biology, psychology, sociology, and politics, this book will be of interest to students and scholars of these disciplines alike.

Michael Robbins is a psychoanalyst, member of the American and International Psychoanalytic Societies, former professor of Clinical Psychiatry at Harvard Medical School, and author of 5 previous books and more than 40 articles in refereed journals.

WHAT MAKES HUMANS UNIQUE

Evolution and the Two Structures of Mind

Michael Robbins

Designed cover image: Flashvector © Getty Images

First published 2024
by Routledge
4 Park Square, Milton Park, Abingdon, Oxon OX14 4RN

and by Routledge
605 Third Avenue, New York, NY 10158

Routledge is an imprint of the Taylor & Francis Group, an informa business

© 2024 Michael Robbins

The right of Michael Robbins to be identified as author of this work has been asserted in accordance with sections 77 and 78 of the Copyright, Designs and Patents Act 1988.

All rights reserved. No part of this book may be reprinted or reproduced or utilised in any form or by any electronic, mechanical, or other means, now known or hereafter invented, including photocopying and recording, or in any information storage or retrieval system, without permission in writing from the publishers.

Trademark notice: Product or corporate names may be trademarks or registered trademarks, and are used only for identification and explanation without intent to infringe.

British Library Cataloguing-in-Publication Data
A catalogue record for this book is available from the British Library

Library of Congress Cataloging-in-Publication Data
Names: Robbins, Michael, M.D., author.
Title: What makes humans unique : evolution and the two structures of mind / Michael Robbins.
Description: Abingdon, Oxon ; New York, NY : Routledge, 2024. |
Includes bibliographical references and index.
Identifiers: LCCN 2023017569 (print) | LCCN 2023017570 (ebook) |
ISBN 9781032564913 (hardback) | ISBN 9781032564920 (paperback) |
ISBN 9781003435785 (ebook)
Subjects: LCSH: Mind and body. | Reason. | Evolution. |
Psychoanalysis.
Classification: LCC BF161 .R633 2024 (print) | LCC BF161 (ebook) |
DDC 128/.2—dc23/eng/20230624
LC record available at https://lccn.loc.gov/2023017569
LC ebook record available at https://lccn.loc.gov/2023017570

ISBN: 9781032564913 (hbk)
ISBN: 9781032564920 (pbk)
ISBN: 9781003435785 (ebk)

DOI: 10.4324/9781003435785

Typeset in Optima
by codeMantra

To three deceased men who profoundly influenced my professional development: James Winn, a high school teacher who took an interest in a clueless young man; Robert Grose, psychology professor at Amherst College; and Elvin Semrad, who was so effective reducing psychoanalysis to living and loving that I and many of my fellow graduate students in clinical psychology at Harvard defected to go to medical school and become psychoanalysts, and as a consequence Harvard fired him.

CONTENTS

Acknowledgments	*xi*
Preface	*xiii*

1 Psychoanalysis and the structures of mind 1

2 The mental structure humans share with other primates and the structure that is unique 7

3 History of the concept of two mental structures from psychoanalysis and other disciplines 16

4 The distinctive languages of each mental structure 27

5 The structure common to all species and its manifestations 34

6 Acquisition of the second mental structure during the separation phase of development 39

7 Limitation of the biological theory of evolution in understanding the origins of the second mental structure 46

8 Efforts to fit what makes humans unique into the biological theory of evolution lead to the need for a revision 50

x Contents

9 The origins of social structure from mental structure:
the social organization derived from the primordial structure   55

10 History of the parallel evolution of the second
mental structure and the movement of human social
organization from socio-centric to self-centric   63

11 The structural difference between neurosis and psychosis   73

12 Mental structure, social organization, and the complex
interplay of socially constructive and destructive
phenomena arising from them   91

13 Mental structures and the evolution of homo sapiens   98

References   *105*
Index   *111*

ACKNOWLEDGMENTS

A dialogue with Fred Levine, PhD, a psychoanalytic colleague whose persistent questioning about what I think makes my ideas different from others, led me to crystallize the conceptual foundation of the book. His critical reading of initial efforts helped me to refine it.

PREFACE

This is the first of two books devoted to the complexity of the human mind that distinguishes homo sapiens from other species. Their purpose is to integrate the findings of evolution, primatology, sociology, and cultural anthropology with those of psychoanalysis, and in so doing to expand the scope and usefulness of each of them.

This book elaborates how the human mind is structured, and the companion book, *The Human Difference: Evolution, Civilization – and Destruction* (in press), addresses its unique manifestations. As the title suggests, the second book addresses a subject many people have been reluctant to face: the unique breadth, depth, and virulence of human destructiveness.

This book proposes an alternative to Freud's much criticized but still generally accepted theory of mental structure. Freud based his model of the human mind on the concept of three structures – id, ego, and superego – and the mental energy fueling their dynamic interaction. His conception was limited by his ignorance of the related disciplines of sociology, primatology, cultural anthropology, and most notably evolution, which were then in their infancy. The result has been isolation of the discipline of psychoanalysis from other scientific disciplines. One of the consequences is the fundamental and perplexing problem usually thought of as the mysterious leap from the mind to the body.

Contrary to what many continue to believe, all animate creatures, probably including forms of what we think of as vegetative life, are "intelligent," in the broadest sense of the term. It is easier for us to comprehend the mental similarity of other life forms the closer they resemble ourselves, most notably some of the creatures we have domesticated as pets and therefore live with and observe closely, and other primates. Human infants and small

xiv Preface

children share this biologically determined and constrained primordial form of intelligence with many other species.

The human mind is unique among species, however. The biological basis of the difference is known as neoteny, the prolonged period of post-natal immaturity that necessitates an extensive period of learning from caregivers. During the learning process, humans acquire a second mental structure, reflective representational thought, that in turn leads to the acquisition of complex knowledge. As a result, humans are the only species capable of intergenerational transmission and accumulation of knowledge independent of biology.

The pages to come elaborate the nature and complexity of the human difference and conclude with a discussion of the implications of the unique structuring of mind for us as individuals, as a society, and for our ultimate survival or extinction as a species.

1

PSYCHOANALYSIS AND THE STRUCTURES OF MIND

Much psychoanalytic literature has been devoted to elaboration and criticism of Freud's metapsychology, particularly his structural model of the psyche. This book takes the further step of proposing a more useful conception of the structure of mind. The mental structures that are proposed and their significance have no resemblance to those that Freud described, although the lineage of the ideas can be traced to other of his writings. There are major problems with Freud's structural model and various efforts that have been made to amend it. The solution is not to jettison the concept of mental structures, but rather to recognize its importance and propose that there are more useful ones. The book describes how the human mind is comprised of two structures, one primordial, that humans share with many other animals; and another, reflective representational thought, that uniquely distinguishes humankind from other species. Freud's proposal that there are two mental processes, primary and secondary, is the antecedent of the model of mind I propose.

Psychoanalysis is a complicated discipline because it amalgamates and often conflates an evolving theory of mind that aspires to be scientific, a clinical method for treating disturbed persons based on the evolving theory of mind, and the capacity to form a good human relationship that is an essential part of any effective therapeutic process. All this is further complicated by Freud's decision not to distinguish his creative ideas from the quasi-religious movement he created to control and perpetuate them.

The aspect of psychoanalysis that aspires to be a science – and a discussion of whether psychoanalysis is or can aspire to be a science is beyond the scope of this book – is the study of how mind works and the gradual movement from hypothesis and theory to accretion of useful knowledge. The primary data is

DOI: 10.4324/9781003435785-1

2 Psychoanalysis and the structures of mind

the study of the minds of human beings, usually persons who are disturbed enough to need help, in a clinical setting whose basic purpose is not study but therapy. The study is enriched by clinical research with infants and children. Adequate testing of hypotheses in a therapeutic setting is problematic, because the privacy of the clinical relationship does not lend itself to traditional forms of objectification and verification that depend on having multiple researchers study the same phenomenon.

Recognizing both the problems and the opportunities inherent in the unique aspects involved in the acquisition of psychoanalytic knowledge, the first question that needs to be addressed is what is a mental structure? In ordinary discourse, references to structure evoke concrete images, like the steel skeleton of a building under construction. For most psychoanalysts, the concept of mental structure is synonymous with Freud's tripartite model of mental structure. These, in turn, are usually referred to concretely as "the" ego, id, and superego. Mental structures are not concrete although efforts have been made to reduce mind to its material brain substrate. Mental structures are usually described as collections of functions or agencies of mind that operate as a system. An analogy might be a symphony orchestra and the symphonies it plays. A composition, already indeterminate as it is up to the musicians to translate the musical notation into sounds, may be played by a group of musicians of varying interests and abilities, and a conductor with a particular style and idiosyncratic ideas about how to translate the notations into music. Performances of the same piece at different times, in different places, and with different personnel are all different from one another but can be recognized as the same piece of music. Similar systematic fluidity is characteristic of structures of the mind.

Freud's structural model was not an original idea. It seems to have been derived from the ancient Greeks – Socrates and his student Plato – 2,500 years earlier. Socrates lectured about the soul and coined the term "psyche", that has become a part of psychoanalytic thinking, to describe it. Plato separated psyche (soul) from body (soma). He conceived of soul as a tripartite structure, comprising logistikon (thought or reason), thumoedes, spirit or passion (affects including anger), and the basest animal or appetitive part, epithumeikon. He located these parts of the soul in specific body areas: reason in the head or mind, passion in the chest, and the base appetites in the stomach. The passionate and appetitive parts are described as sensory-perceptual, somatic, sensual, concrete, unbounded, and responsible for dreaming, very much like Freud's primary process that is the underpinning of the primordial mental structure I propose. Like Freud's concept of primary process, Plato believed these parts comprise the mental operation of childhood. In the *Phaedrus*, he used the analogy of a team of two horses, one more spirited and the other more unruly, controlled by a charioteer. His writing also presaged the aspect of this book that relates mental structure to social structure. In the

Republic, he used the analogy of three classes of society, the ruling class, the military, and ordinary citizens. Justice was described as the state in which the parts function in harmony. In 1781, Immanuel Kant also postulated a tripartite model of individual mind, consisting of reason, understanding, and sensibility, which resembles Freud's superego, ego, and id, respectively.

In Arlow and Brenner's 1964 reference work *Psychoanalytic Concepts and the Structural Theory*, "the" id is the energizing part of mind based on instinctual wishes (drives); "the" ego is the executive part, a group of mental operations LaPlanche and Pontalis described in 1973 as an agency. On p. 39, Arlow and Brenner list 11 such functions including thought, language, and defenses. Ego arises out of good early experience with caregivers. The superego is defined as "the group of mental functions that have to do with ideal aspirations and with moral commands and prohibitions" that arises out of "violent mental conflicts of the phallic-Oedipal phase." The similarity between Freud's ego and Plato's logistikon (thought or reason) as an organized collection or system of governing functions is evident. It seems to encompass the energy that Plato assigned to the other two systems, passion and appetite. Superego appears to be another aspect of governing function that arises later out of conflict. Arlow and Brenner believe that the primary process is not a structure in itself, but is characteristic of the way mind works, "mobility of cathexis," that accounts for things like displacement, condensation, and absence of contradiction. They assert that what they call thinking is not synonymous with the secondary process, and that the primary process can be found in thinking. In this, I believe they confuse the fact that language is used differently in primordial mentation, for example, the language characteristic of infancy, than it is in reflective representational thought.

The concept of mental structure I propose in this book is very different than that in the structural model as explicated by Arlow and Brenner and others. The differences noted above will be elaborated throughout the book. For now, I begin, in both an ontogenetic and sequential sense, by noting how Freud's theory of instinct and drive is both inadequate and from an evolutionary perspective incorrect. His concepts of ego and superego are encompassed in the structure I call reflective representational thought, which resembles Freud's secondary process. These reflect the human difference; what sets us apart from other species. In the structural model I propose, there is an antecedent primordial mental structure that humans are born with and share with other species including our primate ancestors. Freud was partly aware of it when he formulated the primary process model in 1900 in *The Interpretation of Dreams*, but he did not fully understand its nature and its significance as the initial structural underpinning of mind in humans, and the only mental structure in other animate species.

The relationship between mental structures and neural structures is another subject that Freud did not understand and therefore was unable to

4 Psychoanalysis and the structures of mind

take adequate account of when he formulated his economic and structural models. Freud understood the fundamental importance of biology and its neural expression. His significant statements on the subject came at the very beginning of his career and then half a century later at the very end. In 1895, he expressed the hope that someday direct causal connections would not only be revealed but that a substantial neural model would replace the more hypothetical one:

> The deficiencies in our experience would probably vanish if we were already in a position to replace the psychological terms by physiological or chemical ones…we may expect it [biology] to give us the most surprising information and we cannot guess what answers it will return in a few dozen years to the questions we have put to it.
>
> *(1920, p. 60)*

In 1940, in the course of a general summary of his formulation of psychoanalysis, he had shifted position and wrote: "Everything that lies between is unknown to us, and the data do not include any relation between these two terminal points of our knowledge" (1940, p. 144). In other words, he no longer believed there is any connection between these systems, either reductive or causal. However, he did not understand the science of evolution, then in its infancy, and did not comprehend what the biology driving humans is and how it manifests itself psychologically, in the activity of mind. He did not know that and how it differs from that in other animals. He did not understand how the biology of instinct is causally linked to the mental functions that he referred to as drives, and he postulated mind registers as wishes. His theory fails to explain how what he believed to be the instinctual basis of life (Eros) and death (Thanatos) becomes mental ideation.

As a result of Freud's limitations and despite his optimistic prediction, five times the 20 years he envisioned have elapsed and one of the most perplexing problems in psychoanalysis, that Felix Deutsch called the mysterious leap from the mind to the body but many now think of as the leap from biological body processes to mental function, remains unsolved. Psychoanalysts have approached this problem from the two seemingly opposite perspectives of mind and brain. Numerous theorists have recognized that primordial mind is undeveloped, early sensation and expression of self is somatic, and studied how maturation involves development of mental processes that control and express what the body is "saying." Others have worked from the perspective of neuroscience leading to the discipline of neuro-psychoanalysis that attempts to find neural correlates that underly mental processes.

The book starts from the perspective of evolution of species and synthesizes these two approaches. Despite some of Freud's regrets and desires, psychoanalysis developed as the study of mind separate both from biology, and from the evolution of homo sapiens as a species whose mental processes and their manifestations as civilization and culture are unique and make humans different from all other species. The book links findings of evolution theory and psychoanalytic theory of mind by describing why and how humans acquire a second mental process that distinguishes us from other species and how that process accounts for the transition from reflexive biologically-driven mentation, common to all species and to human infants, to sophisticated mental process.

Mental structures and their maturation in humans are qualitatively different than in other species because of what evolutionary biologists call neoteny (Gould, 1977), the relative immaturity of human infants at birth and the lengthy period of dependency on caregivers it necessitates. The consequence of this necessity is a process of learning from caregivers that has produced a unique structure of human mind, reflective representational thought, that in turn has led to acquisition of knowledge and its intergenerational transmission, an independent evolutionary force.

Before proceeding to the substance of the book, I would like to describe some of the concepts involved in understanding the structures of mind, their development, and functional dynamics. I owe a conceptual debt to Heinz Werner, a developmental psychologist, who described structural development in humans clearly in 1940. He writes of an initial

> "…unity of world and ego. The world is separated only slightly from the ego; it is predominantly configured in terms of the emotional needs of the self (egomorphism)" (1940, p. 361). He says "…in different types of primitive mentality psychological functions are more intimately fused, that is, more syncretic, than in the advanced mentality…. In advanced forms of mental activity we observe thought processes which are quite detached from the concrete sensori-motor perceptual and affective sphere. In the primitive mentality, however, thought processes always appear as more or less perfectly fused with functions of a sensori-motor and affective type. It is this absence of a strict separation of thought proper from perception, emotion and motor action which determines the significance of so-called concrete and affective thinking…characteristic examples of syncretic activity" (p. 213). In the syncretic state "…the object is represented not explicitly, but implicitly by means of motor-affective behavior."
>
> *(1940, p. 250)*

He writes "In the young child, however, there is a relatively close connection between perception and imagery" (1940, p. 389). He adds "For the child the reality of the dream and of the waking world are relatively undifferentiated. At this stage waking reality often exhibits some of the characteristics of the dream" (1948, p. 391). Werner's concepts of integration and differentiation are essential to an understanding of the formation of psychic structure. In healthy maturation, while the primordial mental structure and function remains available and essential throughout life, it is employed selectively. The mature mind is characterized by a sense of self (Robbins, 2011, 2018a, 2018b) and by the capacity to experience and resolve intrapsychic conflict between contradictory, opposing, and more or less socially adaptable ideas and associated affects. Pathological development that is arrested in the early attachment-separation phase prior to structural acquisition of reflective thought leads to what is called psychosis. The pathology Freud called neurosis, and related disturbances of character and behavior, generally develops subsequent to acquisition of reflective thought, what Werner describes as differentiation and integration of the personality, and the resulting capacity to experience and resolve intrapsychic conflict. The result is mature resolution of conflicts and acquisition and use of defense mechanisms that lead to inhibitions, symptoms, and maladaptive deformations of character.

2

THE MENTAL STRUCTURE HUMANS SHARE WITH OTHER PRIMATES AND THE STRUCTURE THAT IS UNIQUE

Most of us do not live in the jungle or around other large natural animal habitats. With the move to "civilization" and away from a world where species naturally co-mingled, our view of animals came to be divided into domesticated species that we have taken from their natural environments and in a sense imprisoned, and with whom we are familiar, and "jungle" creatures of imagination, believed to be "wild" or even "savage." This gulf has been fueled by long-standing religious beliefs that divide "man," made in the image of God, endowed with intelligence, language, moral reason, and soul, from so-called "lower" bestial forms of life.

In recent decades, the pendulum of belief has begun to swing to the opposite extreme, perhaps because so many of us have, depend on and observe our "pets." Now many people believe that other animals and a variety of non-animal species have personalities and think, feel, and communicate much as humans do, although they lack the speech and language with which to express themselves. In 2017, for example, Franz de Waals published the best-selling book whose underlying assumption is laid out in unmistakable terms in its title: "Are we smart enough to know how smart animals are?" Perhaps the truth lies somewhere in between these polarities. Humans are unique. But that does not necessarily make us better, or superior – just different. We are all also alike insofar as we share a primordial mental structure that is adaptive in the contexts in which it is utilized, and that is what this chapter is mostly about.

In recent years "civilized" humans have returned to nature by the back door as explorers, including creating a new discipline of animal research that incorporates natural observation, which has become almost synonymous with Jane Goodall. She observed that chimps in their natural environment and

DOI: 10.4324/9781003435785-2

8 The mental structure common to all animals

social habitat are caring, social creatures. She observed nuanced signaling interactions involving gesture and facial expression among members of chimp families and between community members and understood them in terms of social organization based on emotional bonding and learning.

Naturalistic observation has produced remarkable anecdotes about animal intelligence. A female chimp in her natural habitat in Zambia began to adorn herself by keeping a blade of grass in her ear, and others in her tribe imitated her and transmitted the behavior to the next generation. Amalia Bastos, et al published a study (2021) of a Kea parrot to whom they gave the human name Bruce, whose upper beak, which is essential for feather preening and cleaning, must have been destroyed when he was young. He had taught himself to hold a small stone between his tongue and lower beak in order to accomplish the task.

Chimp and bonobo researchers have taken the next step of employing spoken language, visual symbols, and use of computerized equipment to test captive primates and try to understand these processes in greater detail. The result is the realization that primates possess the capacity for primordial mentation, a mental structure they share with human infants and small children. Here is some of what they have discovered.

Most research has been on primates that most closely resemble humans. Research on intelligence consists of studies of self-awareness, use of language, emotional expressiveness, and relationship attachment and bonding.

While examples abound of intelligence among dolphins, elephants, crows and parrots, and other creatures – recently an octopus – most studies have concentrated on language, as an expression of, or window into mind (Robbins, 2018b). Sue Savage Rumbaugh, Allen and Beatrix Gardner, Francine Patterson (a student of the Gardners), and Herbert Terrace and associates are among those who have made notable efforts to teach primates to use language. From time to time, we read remarkable examples of their success.

Of course, chimps in their natural habitat do not speak, write, or use signs or symbols, so investigating their language capabilities is challenging, and it is difficult to know in what context to interpret conclusions. Mind is the product of brain, the product of its capacities and its constraints. The brain of our closest animal ancestor, the chimpanzee, is a quarter the size of the human brain, whereas its average body weight is about three-quarters as much as that of humans. However, size and intelligence are not directly correlated. Chihuahuas and several species of fish have bigger brains proportional to their body than humans. Sea lions have a larger frontal cortex than baboons. Lemurs have larger frontal cortex proportional to body weight than humans. Specialization of function yields other useful information. Area 10 is one of the cortical areas of the frontal lobe involved in higher cognitive functions such as the undertaking of initiatives and the planning of future actions. It is larger in the human brain relative to the rest of the brain than it is in chimps.

The mental structure common to all animals **9**

This suggests that the neural substrates supporting cognitive functions associated with this part of the cortex enlarged and became specialized during hominid evolution. In addition, other primates lack vocal apparatus and the Broca's cortex to control it that enables and supports human speech.

Cerebral differences notwithstanding, there are remarkable examples of primates who have successfully been taught the rudiments of language– if its definition is limited to a system of functionally useful signs and signals as is the case with the primordial structure and its language– as is elaborated in subsequent chapters. Bonobos learn primordial language best, and Kanzi is reputed to be a star among bonobos. Sue Savage-Rumbaugh and her team (2001) tried unsuccessfully to train Kanzi's adoptive mother to use a keyboard with signs that the computer vocalized as words when pressed, accompanied by presentation of the object or action they represent. Kanzi was an observer during his mother's educational failure. By age six, which is approximately the time of full maturation for a bonobo, he had acquired a vocabulary of 200 words and was able to use them in instrumental ways combined with gestures or with other words. There are videos of Kanzi injecting his stuffed dog with a syringe in response to the command "Give the dog a shot." On another occasion, Savage-Rumbaugh used the computer to say, "Can you make the dog bite the snake?" Kanzi searched among a collection of objects until he found a toy dog and a toy snake, put the snake in the dog's mouth, and used his thumb and finger to close the dog's mouth over the snake. "Dog," for Kanzi, had a concrete meaning as a particular one of his toys. Kanzi was asked to identify 35 different items, and his success rate was 93 percent. On another occasion, he was asked over 400 questions and responded correctly to more than 70 percent. Kanzi and others who also learned the relationship between button pressing, vocalized words, objects, and actions, were housed in a specially equipped dwelling that had button-operated doors, a video with DVDs that could be selected with buttons, and a kitchen with vending machine where they could get snacks. They developed their own taste and aesthetic preferences, and, for example, particularly enjoyed DVDs starring primates interacting with humans, such as Tarzan films.

Washoe, a chimpanzee, was taught to sign by the Gardners. Washoe was able to transfer the sign for the adverb "more" that she had learned in relation to tickling, to other activities she wished to repeat, and to combine several signs in novel ways to make phrases to convey wishes. Washoe adopted an infant chimp named Loulis, who was not trained by humans, but acquired more than 50 signs by watching its mother and other trained chimps. The investigators concluded that this instrumental language learning was spontaneously being transmitted from one generation to the next, analogous to the earliest stages of humans learning and use of language.

Francine Patterson set out to teach ASL to a gorilla named Koko in 1972. She claimed Koko comprehended approximately 1,000 ASL signs and 2,000

10 The mental structure common to all animals

English words, but the comprehension was concrete, lacking in grammar and symbolic capacity. She likened Koko's development to that of a two- or three-year-old human child.

Herbert Terrace and his associates at the Central Washington University Chimp and Human Communication Institute (CHCI) were able to teach a family of chimps the use of sign language and the ability to converse with one another and their trainers by constructing meaningful sequences, one said to be seven signs in length. They appeared to communicate with one another about aspects of their lives together, such as signaling the wish to play games, like tickling and chasing. They were able to make simple category generalizations like small children do; for example, "dog" was used to designate all dog-like creatures (but not dog-like toys). One chimp referred to a watermelon as "drink fruit."

These observations demonstrate that although this kind of learning is not a natural part of chimp repertory, when captive in a human environment and exposed to opportunities as infants they possess the primordial mental structure that enables them to learn more or less as human infants do, use the learning socially among themselves and then "teach" their own infants and pass the knowledge on to subsequent generations. However, if these chimps were returned to their natural habitat where the learned knowledge was of no immediate instrumental value, it would soon be lost as it is not transmitted directly by biology.

Franz de Waals emphasizes the contextual embeddedness or concreteness of animal learning. In his books, he gives numerous examples of birds and animals who make instrumental use of environmentally available objects as tools to achieve an anticipated goal that involves food provision. This is not the design and manufacture of sophisticated tools that characterize a member of homo sapiens who is not fettered by the imperative need to have dinner. He claims their intelligence is not sophisticated by human standards because what we call intelligence would be of no use in their world, but I think the problem is broader. The research summarized above indicates their intelligence is equally limited when they are held captive in a more human world.

Our primate ancestors once lived in "that world" and somehow moved beyond situational learning to satisfy less immediate visceral appetites to more complex "needs" like building spacecraft to explore the universe. One of de Waals' examples designed to illustrate the similarity between humans and chimps is that humans might have as much difficulty distinguishing chimp faces as chimps have distinguishing those of humans. However, once again he is illustrating a mind that is concrete, immediate, and stimulus bound. There was no immediate need for humans to have computers, fly in the sky or visit the moon, but that did not prevent humans from developing the capacity to imagine such possibilities and inventing the means to actualize them.

The mental structure common to all animals **11**

Turning to self-awareness, another attribute of intelligence that has been tested in animals, in the 1970s Gordon Gallup devised a now widely copied experiment using a mirror as research tool. He documented stages in animal development of self-awareness: social expressions, gestures, and sounds designed to elicit responses from another animal; physical inspection of the mirror to determine whether it is another animal; and finally, what he called the "mark test" in which the animal spontaneously touches a mark that has been made on its body that could only be visible with the aid of the mirror. This final action is believed to connote self-awareness. According to his criteria, Dolphins and some whales, Chimpanzees and some monkeys, elephants, magpies, and even ants possess this critical ability.

This is a clever experiment, but I believe that the conclusion that the self-awareness that is demonstrated is like that of adult humans is unjustified. It is more like that of the initial objectification of oneself human infants and small children copy from parent treatment of them but does not indicate the acquisition of thought and language reflective of a sense of self and other separateness or of an inner life distinct from external reality. In other words, the animal becomes aware of itself as an object, a "thing," not a separate cogitating subject like itself. I will return to this point throughout the book as I elaborate the hypothesis that structural dualism of mind and the associated capacity to appreciate a world (including others) that is separate from oneself is learned by humans as we mature, and that while human infants and other animals share a primordial mental process that enables survival and adaptation to immediate surroundings, reflective representational thought – the substrate of creative thinking beyond the moment – is the unique product of human development and learning.

Self-awareness and language development are related. Some other animals, like human infants in the first couple of years of life, are able to be aware of themselves as objects, but are not able to make the mental leap, signified by development of reflective representational thought, to view themselves as subjects. Infants can point to, name, and reach for objects of need and interest as chimps are able to do using keyboards or buttons labelled with signs. While chimps do not have language, the mirror test indicates that they can develop a similar sense of self-objectification. When infants first learn their names, for example, it is a result of mother referring to them as objects, not selves. In other words, a mother might say "Jane wants x," not "you want x." and the infant will refer to itself by name as well. When small children begin to use "I", it denotes awareness of self as a separate being with an internal mind and things to think *about*. Soon thereafter, they become capable of using second and third person pronouns, indicating awareness other humans are separate selves, not just objects of interest; they have developed reflective thought, a mental activity not available to other animals.

Descartes' statement "I doubt, therefore I think, therefore I am," remains the best simple definition of the self-awareness characteristic of reflective

12 The mental structure common to all animals

representational thought. Noam Chomsky, long the Chair of the linguistics department at MIT as well as a prominent social activist, proposed that the distinguishing characteristic of language is reflective self-awareness, a concept that he called recursion. Steven Pinker, a vocal critic of claims by primate researchers that chimps have acquired language, states that recursion is a procedure that invokes an instance of itself. "...all you need for recursion is an ability to embed a noun phrase within a noun phrase, or a clause within a clause..." (1994). While Pinker is correct in inferring chimps lack this capacity, his and Chomsky's conclusion that "chimp-speak" or "infant-speak" is not language is based on an artificially limited definition of language.

Another claim made by those who maintain that the intelligence of other animals is like that of humans is based on the belief that they are capable of experiencing specific emotions, and that because some animals appear capable of specific recognition of one another and of caregivers after separations, that they remember the way humans do, by calling on mental representations and associated specific feelings. For example, a dolphin in an aquarium who had not seen another captive dolphin in 20 years was observed to be excited to see it when they were reunited. In his most recent book, *Mama's Last Hug*, Franz de Waals describes the deathbed reunion of an aged zoo chimpanzee and the primatologist Jan van Hooff, who had worked with her but had been absent from her life for many years. The listless dying chimp recognized him and reached out to touch him when he approached her. Similar anecdotes are often told about elephants. The reunions are accompanied by shows of what observers call emotion that are considered to be evidence of the capacity for memory and emotional specificity. Naturalistic observers of primates including Jane Goodall and Alison Gopnik, and ethologists such as Carl Safina at Stony Brook, have observed chimps laughing, making deep attachments to kin, and suffering after their losses. This claim of similarity between humans and other primates, however, overlooks the critical distinction between affect, a somatic, physiologic, behavioral expression that, once again, is common to other primates and to human infants, and the capacity to represent and be aware of specific emotions, which is an exclusively mature human attribute. And there is an important distinction between recognition of something or someone familiar that is enacted psychosomatically with gesture, facial expression, and vocalization, signifying an affective experience, and the presence of enduring memory, that depends on continuous mental representation of emotion and thought. Other than short-term searching behavior following loss, for example, there is no evidence the dolphin remembered its fellow, or the chimp Dr. van Hooff. And no one would claim that these creatures "knew" the feeling or feelings they were having that corresponded with their behavior. An example from the work of Daniel Everett, the linguist and anthropologist who studied the Pirahã tribe, may help to clarify the distinction between constant representation that is indicative both of memory

The mental structure common to all animals **13**

and anticipation, and recognition of something psychosomatically familiar that has not achieved mental representational status. Everett observed that the tribespeople became fascinated with the float planes on which he and his family and others arrived and departed. For a short time after a plane arrived many of them carved models of planes from wood, but the activity was transient as was any sense from their language that they retained memory of the event or that they anticipated a future arrival. When another plane arrived, they recognized it with excitement and appropriate language, but the recognition was bound to the stimulus, the sequence was repeated, and once again there was no indicated the event had been remembered and another coming anticipated.

The capacity for recognition on presentation of something that is familiar along with the expression of appropriate affect in the form of face-making, gesturing, and bodily sensations is very different from stable memory and awareness of the accompanying emotions, although the immediate behavioral consequences may appear to be the same. Human infants develop the sensory-perceptual capacity to recognize mother, in contrast to other caregivers, sometime late in the first year of life; and to respond to her with facial expression, gesture, and vocalization; but there is no indication the infant is able to form and sustain an image of mother in her absence, or of an emotion (love or anger, for example) in relation to her. When the infant is hungry and cries it seems to need food rather than to want the remembered mother who feeds it. Such mental elements emerge later, as the language of pronoun representation reflects the movement from a concrete instrumental mind in which mother is equated with need satisfaction to one in which she is a remembered separate other person in the absence of felt need. It is not until well along in childhood that infants gradually stop expressing themselves by crying, gesticulating, and making other vocal sounds that sensitive adults can identify as expressions of emotions such as desire, fear, anger, pleasure, or despair, and with the help of adults around them begin to talk in the mental language of specific emotions about themselves and of desire for specific remembered others. It is no accident that the primitive language of expletives is full of gastrointestinal, urogenital, and respiratory references that convey affects, rather than in language expressive of specific emotions.

It appears that the mental activity of other animals most closely resembles the mental activity of human infants and very small children, and that humans develop a second mental structure and predominant use of reflective representational thought. The basis for the distinction between humans and other species begins with genetics and biology, but the ultimate causal factor is psychosocial. Human infants are extremely immature at birth in comparison to the young of other species. They require a lengthy period of extrauterine dependency while they mature, whereas the young of other animal species are mature and capable of functioning independently at or soon after

14 The mental structure common to all animals

birth because their behavior is for the most part biologically programmed and stereotypic. Biologists call this distinguishing feature of our species neoteny. An important consequence of the process of learning from caregivers is that there is a broad variation in adult human personality and social structure compared to the relative uniformity of personality and social organization of other adult primates. This variability, in turn, is transmitted and grows from parents to children and from one generation to the next.

Beginning with the biological difference, the chimp brain is 40 percent of its adult size at birth and has reached full size of about 640 cubic centimeters by age seven. By around six chimps are mostly mature and independent. Human babies are born when their brains are less than 30 percent of adult size. While the human brain reaches full size at approximately the same age as the chimp brain, it continues to grow in complexity, especially the prefrontal cortex, until age 20 or 25. The human brain also possesses speech centers that primates lack, that enable complex communication, that in turn facilitates complex learning, beyond the isolated capabilities of a single person.

Chimpanzees are totally dependent on parenting until age two, and partially dependent until age four to six years. At that time, they meet the criteria for adulthood defined as the ability to forage and otherwise take care of themselves, to adapt to the local community, and the achievement of sexual maturity and the ability to reproduce. Strikingly different as this is from human maturation, chimps are late maturers compared to other animal species. Although there is no doubt that other animals learn from interactions with their environment, the balance of learned skill and behavior, on the one hand, and reflexive pre-wired biological response, on the other, is heavily weighted toward the biological and toward developments prior to birth, and the learning is mostly instrumental and immediately environmentally bound.

The long post-partum years of neurobiological and psychosocial maturation that set humans apart from other species require and enable a learning process based on a second mental structure, and intergenerational transmission of knowledge that is unique in the animal kingdom. It creates a psychologically separate sense of self and a focus on individual actualization or self-determination, and a complexity of social organization, unknown in other species.

The knowledge accumulated by transmission from human generation to generation that enables individual development and powers actualization of each person's unique abilities has produced the complexity and sophistication of human civilization and culture, which transcends biological survival and immediate community maintenance. Humans are able to learn from past experience and use the knowledge to create novel experiences in ways that transcend simple instrumental processes that satisfy immediate needs. This learning involves the capacity for conscious reflection and choice that enables us to expand our understanding and control over ourselves and the world around us. It enables us to transmit a significant amount of what has been learned to subsequent generations via education of our young during their period of immature dependency. But there is a dark side to this remarkable achievement. It also generates destructive clashes between social groups and creates learned destructiveness from disturbed interactions with caregivers. We humans have been to a significant extent freed from the imperative that biology is destiny but the price we pay is that our knowledge also creates the possibility of a destiny that is more difficult to predict, both more creative and more ominous.

3

HISTORY OF THE CONCEPT OF TWO MENTAL STRUCTURES FROM PSYCHOANALYSIS AND OTHER DISCIPLINES

Freud may have been the first in modern times to propose that the human mind is comprised of structures, but the concept dates back at least to ancient Greece. Unfortunately, Freud was unaware of the foundational significance for the structure of mind of his proposal of primary and secondary processes, and instead constructed his tripartite structural model of the mind – id, ego, and superego – on a proposal first formulated in ancient Greece by Plato, and subsequently elaborated by Kant.

In 1900, Freud described the primary process, derived from his study of dreaming, that ontologically precedes the development of what he called secondary process thought. He focused on the collection of mental operations that characterize it, not on the fact that this collection or system meets the criteria of a mental structure.

Freud believed the primary process, the forerunner of the concept of a primordial structure that I propose, underlies the mentation of infants whereas the secondary process, which generally meets the criteria of the second mental structure unique to humans, reflective representational thought, is the mental process (or structure) of adults.

Perhaps because his understanding of the primary process came from the study of dreams, and dreams occur when people are asleep; and because persons who function according to the primary process lack reflective awareness or "consciousness" of their minds; he believed the process and the phenomena derived from it are unconscious in the sense of being unknowable in a direct sense. He did recognize that it is the mental structure common to infants and small children, but he did not pause to reflect about whether it is accurate to consider their mentation unconscious. Or, to put it differently, a person can be conscious without "knowing" it when in fact its characteristics

DOI: 10.4324/9781003435785-3

are directly observable. Freud's fateful decision has lent an air of mystery and unknowability to this basic mental activity. He believed unconscious activity could only be inferred indirectly from pathological behaviors and "symptoms" derived from it, like one can never know directly what goes on beneath the earth but can only infer it from periodic earthquakes or eruptions. And he did not challenge the implication of his belief for the question of whether infants and small children are "unconscious."

Derivatives of the primordial mental structure are conscious in a different way than reflective thought, which implies the Cartesian capacity to introspect, and the awareness that there is a subjective "I" and a separate objective "thou." While there appears to be an "I" in dreams, in the sense of an experiencing subject, and there are "others," as well, the "I" is not a reflective "I" but an illusion of participation in a drama that feels real. And the "thou" is not another "real" person with whom the dreamer is interacting, as in waking life, but a depiction of an aspect of the dreamer's mind. In other words, in a dream that is experienced as an action drama there is no differentiation of self from other and if there is no reflective self and separate phenomenology for it to contemplate the result is simply a different kind of conscious state.

Freud discovered the primary process through waking thoughtful contemplation of the nature and significance of his own dreams. He described the characteristics of the primary process as displacement, condensation, and absence of contradiction. These terms were his way of saying that mental contents or ideas, and related experiences, that are separate and distinct from one another in waking life, driven by what he called the secondary process, are not differentiated from one another in the primary process. The primary process creates a sensory-perceptual identity; a false sense of reality unfolding that, as he noted, resembles hallucination and delusion in waking life.

The major feature of the primary process is absence of differentiation between mind and world. The primary process creates a narrative linked not by elements of logic, consensual reality, and sense of time, but by predominant affects moods or feeling states. Things are put together that would not ordinarily happen in real life because they make no "logical" sense. As there is no reflective thought and no realistic distinction between mental elements, the dream itself is concrete, not symbolic, a fact that contradicts another of Freud's beliefs that still have a major hold on psychoanalytic theory. Symbolic understanding can be created from a dream by reflective thought once the dreamer awakens and emerges from the dream state. Much of Freud's therapeutic method depends on doing so, but that requires that we recognize (differentiate) that we have had a dream, laboriously translate the imagery and actions into a thoughtful narrative about which we can reflect, and then look for symbolic meaning in that context.

Since Freud, other psychoanalysts have described processes similar to his primary process, and a couple have contrasted the more immature function

18 History of the concept of two mental structures

with a more mature one, but none has suggested a model of dual mental structure that might supplant his tripartite model.

Although Klein and her followers did not recognize and acknowledge their debt to Freud, perhaps because of the contentious political atmosphere that culminated in the so-called "Controversial Discussions" in the UK during World War II, they also articulated a theory of two mental processes or structures. Klein postulated the unintegrated and undifferentiated paranoid-schizoid position characterized by splitting (lack of integration) and phantasy (a concrete, somatic, enactive process). While there is no reference to the primary process in Klein's writings, in 1946 she conjoined her concept of phantasy, the mental process of the paranoid-schizoid position, with the adjective "unconscious." Most of the references to phantasy of Susan Isaacs, as well as those of Hannah Segal, Klein's most important explicators, are similarly coupled with the adjective "unconscious."

Isaacs (1948) offers a particularly eloquent description of phantasy as a somatic process different from and antecedent to conceptual thought. It is concrete and enactive rather than symbolic and reflective, sensory-perceptual-somatic-motor, undifferentiated and unintegrated in the sense implied by projective identification. It creates a hallucinatory-delusional sense of actualization. The mind of phantasy is somatic; gastrointestinal and urogenital; based on the belief that what is "good" can be ingested and what is "bad" can be excreted or eliminated. Need is experienced and enacted orally as somatic tropism toward the mother (breast) that is undifferentiated from a state of satisfaction (goodness), and frustration elicits somatic-psychic excretory responses that are equally undifferentiated from parts of the object (badness). States of incipient and actual satisfaction are experienced as an omnipotent (undifferentiated) hallucinatory/delusional belief that Klein named the "good" breast, while states of frustration and rage are protectively identified in the other as belief in a destroyed/destroying (persecutory) "bad" breast. In contrast to Klein and most Kleinians, Isaacs acknowledges that:

> The earliest and most rudimentary phantasies, bound up with sensory experience, and being affective interpretations of bodily sensations, are naturally characterized by those qualities which Freud described as belonging to the 'primary process': lack of co-ordination of impulse, lack of sense of time, of contradiction, and of negation. Furthermore, at this level, there is no discrimination of external reality. Experience is governed by 'all or none' responses and the absence of satisfaction is felt as a positive evil. Loss, dissatisfaction or deprivation are felt in sensation to be positive, painful experiences.
>
> *(1948, p. 87)*

Matte-Blanco (1975, 1988) described two forms of logic (his term for mental activity) that he called asymmetric and symmetric. Asymmetric logic is the

History of the concept of two mental structures **19**

equivalent of reflective recursive thought. His description of symmetric logic bears much resemblance to Freud's primary process. Like Freud, he believed it to be unconscious, only inferable by its effects on asymmetric logic, even though the process he described is directly observable.

In recent years theorists with relational and attachment theory orientations have produced a substantial literature designed to explicate the area of mental life Freud referred to as unconscious processes that is not defensively repressed but is not available to reflective conscious awareness. For the most part, this group has described the relevant processes in terms of absence of symbolic representation of somatic-motoric-sensory-perceptual experience; what the body knows but the mind has not grasped and articulated. Numerous conceptual labels have been used, the most common being implicit or procedural knowledge. From this large literature, I extract several representative contributions. The Boston Change Process Study Group (BCPSG) (2007) describes implicit or procedural knowing as follows:

> ...we are not referring to the infant's cognitive function, but to the way that physiological and then social/behavioral regulation is carried out between the infant and its caregiver and represented and 'remembered' by the infant... [it] ...guides the moment-to-moment exchanges that occur in any interaction...such as gestures, vocalizations, silences and rhythms.

They go on to say that "...relational knowing is thus a form of representation... [but]...we do not imply a symbolic process" (p. 844). Lyons-Ruth, an attachment theorist, writes:

> ...if development is not primarily about translating primary process into symbolic form, but about developing implicit adaptive procedures for being with others in a wide range of emotionally charged situations, then making the unconscious conscious does not adequately describe developmental or psychoanalytic change.
>
> *(1999, p. 589)*

An implication is that there is a void where mind could be, that the processes involved are somatic and behavioral, representational in the sense of concrete and imagistic, passive and reflexive. Stern *et al.* (1998) describe implicit "...knowing about interpersonal and intersubjective relations, i.e. how to be with someone.... Such *knowings* integrate affect, cognition, and behavioural/interactive dimensions (p. 903)." Emde (1993) states that:

> There is a major amount of nonconscious mental activity that is neither preconscious (i.e., readily accessible to consciousness using recent or working memory) nor defensively excluded (i.e., involving repressed memories

20 History of the concept of two mental structures

or isolated affects) …a variety of organized automatically functioning procedures and rules for guiding behavior in particular contexts.

(p. 415)

These contributions continue to reflect the ambiguity about whether the process is unconscious, conscious in a concrete, stimulus bound, imagistic manner, or conscious in the form of reflective symbolic thought, at the same time that they are a valuable corrective to the tendency to equate unconsciousness with repression, immaturity, and pathology. However, they direct attention to a kind of mental void; behavioral automatisms in the absence of reflective symbolic consciousness rather than the idea of an active and complex conscious mental process that is different from reflective representational thought.

Wilma Bucci (1997, 2000, 2011) addressed this problem and formulated a three-level hierarchy consisting of sub-symbolic non-verbal processing, non-verbal symbolic processing, and verbal symbolic thought. Her model of subsymbolic process encompasses the area of imagistic consciousness. She also describes subsymbolic processes using some of the same terminology as primary process – concrete, non-verbal, sensory-perceptual-motor, and analogical. In seeming contradiction, she describes the process as chaotic rather than lawful and organized, whereas it seems to follow from her own descriptions that it is an orderly process albeit one that is different from reflective thought.

Contributions to mental structure from other disciplines

Others have followed Freud in proposing that human mind works in two qualitatively different ways, most notably the cultural anthropologist Lucien Levy-Bruhl (1923, 1928, 1935), Julian Jaynes (1976), and more recently Daniel Kahneman (2011). From the perspective of cognitive developmental psychology Jean Piaget (1936,1952) developed a four-stage model, the first three stages of which (sensorimotor, pre-operational and concrete operational) bear some resemblance to primordial mental activity.

The work of Piaget and Kahneman is of limited relevance to this discussion. Piaget's model of cognitive development is a sophisticated description of the earliest sensorimotor phase in which mentation is immediate, concrete, and enactive, but his model has no place for the body and affects, which are the antecedents of emotional awareness and representation. In 2011, Kahneman wrote the popular book *Thinking Fast and Slow*. His focus is mostly on practical functional applications of the cognitive process he describes. The similarity to primordial mentation is what he calls fast thinking. It is reflexive and forms beliefs or intuitions that are useful under certain situations that require rapid response, but are impediments in others where contemplative logical thinking and evidence gathering is called for. Bonobos are quicker than older human children in solving some simple problems because they are not burdened with having to think too much about what they are doing.

About a quarter-century after Freud's discovery of the primary process, the cultural anthropologist Lucien Levy-Bruhl wrote a series of books (1923, 1928, 1935) describing the mental activity of tribal people he had observed, calling it primitive because it is not governed by logic, as is the working of the "modern" or European mind of Levy-Bruhl and his fellow anthropologists. He described the inability of primitive mind to differentiate the supernatural from reality, and to recognize and deal with contradictions. But his terminology suggests that he believed he was describing an inferior race, not a different form of mentation that is socially and functionally adaptive under the circumstances in which it occurs. What others call anthropomorphizing or animation of the world he referred to as the process of "mystical participation." Lévy-Bruhl did realize that residues of these "prelogical" elements continue to exist in mature mind along with "logical" ones, or to say it differently, that the two processes are to be found in the ordinary functioning of adult mind. He believed that except for these remnants, mind had evolved over the ages from its original tribal beginnings to European sophistication.

It is important to separate Levy-Bruhl's basic ideas from the cultural bias or judgmentalism prevalent at the time he formulated them. Even in this more enlightened era most of us share the prejudice that logic, science, and technology make us superior, not just different. We tend to believe that "mythology" is a synonym for flawed irrational beliefs, heedless of the fact that the other process plays a significant role in our contemporary life as well, and when it does, we do not call it mythology.

Three-quarters of a century after Freud's discovery of the primary process, Julian Jaynes published the evolutionary hypothesis, he called bicameralism. He speculated that at the evolutionary dawn of homo sapiens, the cerebral hemispheres were not connected. This meant to him that the first humans were unconscious, as the active and emotive behavior originating from the right hemisphere was not recognized and governed by the thoughtful regulation he believed was produced by the left hemisphere as, he believed, the two were not connected. Humans functioned in an anthropomorphic state of undifferentiation from an animated cosmos, a process he called mythopoetic. He believed this mental state to be characteristic of the ancient Greece of the Homeric epics and of pre-Columbian culture, as well as the Old Testament Bible. He further postulated that mental states characteristic of religion, cultism, schizophrenia, and other extreme belief systems are leftovers or "vestiges" of the earlier unconscious bicameral state.

The function he localized to the right hemisphere closely resembles Freud's description of the primary process and that of the primordial mental structure. He described what he calls the loss of the "analog I," or the sense of one's separate self and one's mind; the dissolution of mind-space, by which he means the capacity to introspect or reflect on one's mind; and the absence of what he called narratization; the ability to construct a story about oneself. Along with Descartes and Freud, he defined consciousness as self-awareness, reflection and introspection, the capacity to differentiate inside from outside, and the acquisition of selective control over behavior based upon the capacity to reflect. The functions he ascribed to the left hemisphere resemble those Freud assigned to ego and superego.

Over the course of millennia, Jaynes proposed, the limitations of the bicameral brain caused ancient cultures constructed from this mental limitation to fail, presumably from inadequate regulation, requiring further evolution of the brain that, he believed, took the form of construction of the cerebral commissure, and with it the development of reflective thought and the psychological consciousness necessary to solve the social problems that had caused previous failures.

As the saying goes, right church but wrong pew. His concept of parallel evolution of brain, mind, and society is important, but there is no evidence to support his belief that the two hemispheres were once disconnected. The corpus callosum, the commissure on which his theory rests, so to speak, is present in all placental mammals. In addition, some humans are born without such a commissure, and many of them are high functioning. And his notion of hemispheric separation of function has been replaced by the more sophisticated concept of cerebral networks. Nor is there evidence to support its basis, the hypothesis that ancient tribal and spiritual cultures were any less successful in self-regulation than more contemporary Western culture, unless one defines success as the unique proliferation of population that has led to destruction of other cultures, other species, and an unchecked expansion of the population that threatens destruction of the resources of the planet itself.

Jaynes' hypothesis about mental structure did not gain the lasting respect it deserves because he linked it to incorrect beliefs about biological evolution and cerebral structure and function. That does not diminish the importance of the phenomenology he observed, however.

Freud and Jaynes mistakenly believed the reflective process was conscious whereas the non-reflective process was unconscious. Noam Chomsky (1965, 1978) makes a similar assumption when he claims that any speech or communication that is not recursive and is not expressive of reflective thought does not meet the criterion for language. It follows that Freud and Jaynes believed that infants and small children, whose speech reflects unawareness of having inner lives and of the psychological separateness of self and other are not conscious. This is similar to the assertion of Chomsky and associates that infants do not possess language abilities because they use words and grammar differently than adults.

My conception of the unique dual structures of human mind, then, is not original, but the notion that both are conscious and that they represent the fundamental structures of mind is contrary to prevailing wisdom. It draws on the contributions of others but reformulates the mental processes in a way that clarifies confusion about consciousness, dreaming, childhood, individual development, and human evolution. Mental content cannot be observed directly but must be inferred from behavior, and in humans the behavior that offers deepest insight into the workings of mind is language, therefore much of the ensuing discussion about mind is about language.

Characteristics of the structure responsible for reflective representational thought

The mental activity with which we in the Western world are most familiar, which for the most part governs mature adult behavior and therefore is considered normal, is reflective representational thought. Reflection, that Noam Chomsky calls recursion when it is observed in language, involves the capacity to contemplate one's mental content and to make other forms of differentiation as well. It enables us to differentiate ourselves from others with some accuracy and appreciate others' separateness rather than misperceive them either as aspects of ourselves of which we are not aware, or as alien. It includes the capacity for symbolization, introspection, comparison and contrast, and the sense of a past (memory) and a future (fantasy or imagination). It enables the possibility of contradictory or conflicting thoughts; a kind of mental multitasking not available to persons shackled by belief systems and related reflexive behaviors. Reflective thought is responsible for the development of societies, cultures, and civilization based on implementation of the imagination and creativity of individual members, beyond stimulus-bound need satisfaction and social group adaptation. It enables us to tell stories that we recognize are fictions and not actual events.

Characteristics of the primordial mental structure

The primordial mental activity, by contrast, generates a holistic process that does not distinguish external reality from internal mind; the intrapsychic world of thought from an external world that it animates. It is a here and now process with no sense of time past or future. It is concrete, not symbolic, a world of immediacy and enactment, not reflection and contemplation. The behavior it supports is not based on awareness of choices with separate consequences, or conflicts to be resolved; rather the experience is one of immersion in an ongoing action drama that moves from one event to another. Dreaming is both the developmentally earliest example of primordial mentation and the one least contaminated by immediate reality considerations, and the absence

24 History of the concept of two mental structures

of surprise during the dream itself at the lack of "sensible" transition between one dream image to another indicates the absence of reflective capacity. It is interesting that for members of tribal cultures dreaming and waking life are equivalently conscious and "real." Members of tribal cultures look upon their dreams as actual journeys of discovery, qualitatively similar to physical adventures or journeys in waking life, and do not make the distinction between waking and sleeping (unconscious) states that most of us in Western cultures tend to do. This suggests that the group process in such cultures is mostly based on primordial mentation rather than reflective thought.

The concept of two equivalently "normal" and important mental structures on which we depend runs counter to generally accepted beliefs that the primordial structure is immature, non-functional, or inferior and unsophisticated, probably because it is most conspicuously associated with infancy and early childhood. An interesting functional comparison of the two processes that challenge this belief is that chimpanzees actually perform better on certain cognitive tasks than human children who have reached the age where they are capable of rudimentary reflective thought. The reflection and need to choose that characterizes reflective thought may actually slow children down in performing some cognitive tasks, as their responses no longer have the quickness of reflex. This is the phenomenon Daniel Kahneman (2011) called fast thinking. Another way to look at it is that many complex adult functions that are beyond the capability of other animals, such as driving a car, or performing sophisticated athletic feats are learned from reflective thought but once learned are taken over by the primordial mental process. The initial learning may be slow and laborious. Once learned, however, they become "thoughtless" habits and are done reflexively. We hear expressions like "the driver becomes one with the road." In such instances "thinking too much" can be a problem as it can slow down or disrupt performance. Examples include some baseball players who start to "think too much" about basic activities like throwing and hitting that initially required sophisticated learning and practice but became reflexive. As a consequence of this regressive preoccupation the careers of some star athletes have been ruined. Adults who relate to their children exclusively "by the book" in a logical non-playful way do not make the best parents.

Primordial mentation is not equivalent to delusional thinking and incompetence

Some critics do not accept the fact that primordial mentation can be functionally adaptive and personally and socially constructive, and hence is both normal and in its appropriate context uniquely functional. The noted anthropologist Richard Schweder is one. His doubts are articulated in a critique of Piaget's stage model (2009). He confuses primordial mentation with functional incompetence; how the world is understood with one's ability to function adaptively in the moment. At the same time that their understanding of the world is shaped by primordial mentation, the ability of infants to respond accurately and adaptively to reality by reaching, grasping, bringing things to their mouths, struggling to stand, walk, and then reach perceived goals in terms of destinations in their immediate environment is impressive, limited by their level of motor development, not whether they perceive themselves as separate beings. This important distinction is elaborated in the next chapter and depends on the undifferentiation, interdependence, or symbiosis between infant and caregiver that is normal in infancy.

Another way to gain perspective on the question of sanity and functionality and its relationship to mental structure is to consider members of ancient cultures and of tribal cultures past and present. One would think that if the members of a culture were collectively unrealistic, or to be hyperbolic, delusional, the social system they embraced would be non-functional and would rapidly destruct. But this is hardly the case. We need look no farther than people with passionate religious beliefs in contemporary culture. As for tribal peoples, their beliefs or ways of understanding their relationship with the cosmos appear to have limited relationship to their functional abilities to navigate and survive adaptively and collaboratively in a natural environment. Their adaptive skills in their native environments actually surpass those of most members of contemporary cultures placed in similar situations, who may be logical, reflective, and adept in surviving in technologically sophisticated settings but are as clueless in natural environments lacking in such "civilized" appurtenances as "primitive" persons would be thrown into the midst of big city life.

It may be difficult for some to relate primordial mental activity in humans to the intelligence described in other primates in Chapter 2. However, language skills and speech are not an essential part of primordial mentation. The next chapter describes the normal interaction of mothers and their infants that is called motherese by infant researchers; a complex choreography of eye contact and movement, facial expression, gestures, and at least in the beginning, very little use of language defined narrowly as words. The fundamental characteristic of these interactions is that they are a mutually choreographed, affectively driven, undifferentiated, symbiotic mirroring that is not dependent on language as understood by mature adults.

It is important to remember that primordial mentation is not simply infantile, just as it is not delusional. It normally drives aspects of adult life as well. Parents of infants purposefully, if reflexively, revert to this process in the course of bonding and communicating with them. Artists in the throes of creative process are driven by affect; emotions they do not stop to name. They function in an "altered" enactive state we call the creative process that is undifferentiated from their work and is not logical. A similar mental process is often shared by lovers as well. Cults, rigid belief systems, extreme religious states of ecstasy, all are driven by a similar process. The recent political upheaval between former President Trump and those who disagree with him, and between liberal democrats and the multitude of Republicans who loyally defend what from a logical realistic standpoint are false beliefs about reality and about others, also illustrate a primordial mental process in action. Various examples of expression of the primordial structure including ones that are destructive, ones that are constructive, and ones that are more difficult to categorize in this way such as that of the former president, are presented subsequently in the book.

4

THE DISTINCTIVE LANGUAGES OF EACH MENTAL STRUCTURE

The workings of mind may be inferred from actions, expressions, and gestures but are most accurately reflected in the language and its prosody that we use. The two basic structures of mind – primordial and reflective representational thought – are expressed by the same formal language elements of vocabulary and grammar, although the vocabulary and grammar expressive of the primordial structure is more limited. What the words and grammar designate, however, differs in ways that are not always readily apparent. In other words, one's native and foreign languages can each be employed to express either primordial mentation or reflective thought. The fact that humans employ two different languages and that much of human behavior, individual and social, can be traced to their use, suggests a structural basis for mind. A brief review of the characteristics of each structure precedes the more specific discussion of language.

Characteristics of the reflective representational thought structure

The mental structure used most of the time by mature members of contemporary society is reflective representational thought. Reflective thought is characterized by the capacity to objectify and contemplate the workings of one's mind; one's thoughts, emotions, beliefs, dreams. Noam Chomsky and his associates labelled this capacity as recursion, and they believe it is the single critical distinguishing feature of language. They believe that language is the expression of a biologically based instinct, as Steven Pinker (1998) termed it, that "generates" grammar. They do not accept that the speech characteristic

DOI: 10.4324/9781003435785-4

of what I call primordial mentation is also a manifestation of language, and that the human mind supports two qualitatively different forms of language, because primordial mentation lacks the capacity for recursion. That is another matter (Robbins, 2018b) beyond the scope of this book.

Recursion or reflection enables us to recognize that humans are separate and different and to accept as an essential aspect of human identity the distinction between ourselves and others rather than to view difference as alienating and threatening. We are all alike, more or less, and we are each different in ways deserving of respect. Differentiation is an essential capacity and includes the capacity to compare and contrast; to understand time in the sense of distinctions between past, present, and imagined future; to perceive contradictions and conflicts; and indeed to imagine, have fantasies, and understand that however much we may wish they were reality, they are not. Reflective thought depends on the capacity for symbolization; to see the object at times as a concrete thing in itself and at other times as a representation of something else. As Freud meant, sometimes a cigar is just a cigar; at other times (at least in his theory) it represents a phallus. Such mental multitasking is unique to this mental structure and its language. It enables us to tell stories that we recognize are fictions and not actual events.

Characteristics of the primordial mental structure

Primordial mental activity, by contrast, is a holistic process that does not distinguish external reality from internal mind; the intrapsychic world of thought from an external world that it animates. It is a here and now process of enactment and immediacy with no sense of time past or future. It is concrete, not symbolic. A thing is just a thing. This is why the language of primordial structure is limited; developmentally if we think of it as characteristic of infancy, degraded often into expletives and body part expressions if we consider its maladaptive expression in individual psychosis and less obviously pathological belief systems like some political dogmas and cults. Primordial language expresses a world of immediacy and enactment, not reflection and contemplation. Things just are what they are. The behavior it supports is not based on awareness of choices with separate consequences, or conflicts to be resolved; rather the experience is one of immersion in an ongoing action drama that moves from one event to another.

Dreaming is both the developmentally earliest example of primordial mentation and the one least contaminated by immediate reality considerations. Freud proposed that dreams are based on a distinctive mental activity he called the primary process. He described that process as concrete, enactive, and undifferentiated from reality, yet seemingly unaware of a contradiction he also believed dreams are symbolic. His mistake germinated a century of confusion as he based much of his clinical method on the analysis of dream symbolism. What he failed to take into account is that in order to search our dreams for possible symbolic meaning we must first awaken from the sleeping mental state, reflect on the fact that we have been dreaming, which is not always easy to do, and then laboriously translate the drama in which we have been immersed into a thoughtful if strange narrative about which we can reflect. It is interesting that for members of tribal cultures, who are not burdened with ideas about symbolism, dreaming and waking life are equivalently "real." Therefore, members of tribal cultures look upon their dreams as actual journeys of discovery, qualitatively similar to physical adventures or journeys in waking life, and do not make the distinction between waking and sleeping states that most of us in Western cultures tend to do.

Chapter 2 describes that the primordial mental structure and the language that reflects it is common to many animal species as well as to human infants and small children, although its presence may be more difficult to detect in other animals that lack the capacity for speech communication and therefore cannot provide information through formal language.

The concept of two equivalently "normal" and important mental processes on which we all depend runs counter to generally accepted belief that primordial mentation, a biological expression that commences even prior to birth and that humans share with many other animals, is immature in the sense of being inferior because it is less sophisticated in terms of human development. An interesting functional comparison of the two processes that challenges the simplistic belief that primordial mentation is inferior is that chimpanzees actually perform better on certain cognitive tasks than human children who have reached the age where they are capable of rudimentary reflective thought. The reflection and need to choose that characterizes reflective thought may actually slow children down in performing some cognitive tasks, as their responses no longer have the quickness of reflex. This is the phenomenon Daniel Kahneman called fast thinking. Another way to look at it is that many complex adult functions that are beyond the capability of other animals, such as driving a car, or performing sophisticated athletic feats are learned from reflective thought but once learned are taken over by the primordial mental process. The initial learning may be slow and laborious. Once learned, however, they become "thoughtless" habits and are done reflexively. We hear expressions like "the driver becomes one with the road." In such instances, "thinking too much" can be a problem as it can slow down or disrupt performance. Examples include some baseball players who start to "think too much" about basic activities like throwing and hitting that initially required sophisticated learning and practice but became reflexive. As a consequence of this regressive preoccupation, the careers of some star athletes have been ruined. Looked at from another perspective, the mentation and

30 The distinctive languages of each mental structure

language of primordial mentation is clearly "superior" in other situations. Adults who relate to their children exclusively "by the book" in a logical non-playful way do not make the best parents. Much of the cultural accomplishments of our civilization, especially in the arts, would not exist were humans restricted to logical reflective planning. This is the kind of distinction theorists whose work was described earlier in the chapter refer to as implicit or procedural learning and functioning.

Some do not accept the distinction between what is thought of as sanity and related functional competency in some contexts and the structure and kind of mentation on which it is based. The primordial structure and its language are functionally adaptive and personally and socially constructive in the context within which they normally arise. The noted anthropologist Richard Schweder failed to make this distinction. His doubts are articulated in a critique of Piaget's stage model. He confuses primordial mentation with functional incompetence. But how the world is understood is not always synonymous with one's ability to function adaptively in it. At the same time that their understanding of the world is shaped by primordial mentation, the ability of infants to respond accurately and adaptively to reality by reaching, grasping, bringing things to their mouths, struggling to stand, walk, and then reach perceived goals in terms of destinations in their immediate environment is impressive, limited by their level of motor development, not whether they perceive themselves as separate beings with minds of their own in a world of separate reality and others.

Human infants and small children, and their good-enough caregivers communicate using a language expressive of the primordial structure that is not reflective (lacks recursion), utilizes gesture, facial expression, and action, is affect driven, and consists of fleeting images rather than stable psychic representations. Self and other are not differentiated and therefore elements of infant identity are fluidly interchanged between infant and caretaker. A detailed description of this language, its origins, and its manifestations and evolution in the first years of life are described in the next chapter. Before concluding the discussion of the structural determinants of language an example is presented of the use of the primordial structure and its language that has been remarkably adaptive by a prominent person, the former President of the United States.

Former President of the United States Donald Trump

Former President Donald Trump is an unusual example of how successful someone whose mental structure and associated use of language has not developed beyond its primordial beginnings can be. He has enjoyed remarkable financial, social, sexual, and political success. Almost half the population think he is not just normal, but exceptional.

The distinctive languages of each mental structure **31**

Absence of integration and as a result, narrative full of contradiction and inconsistency abound. It appears to others he is continuously lying in order to suit his belief of the moment and maintain the sense that he alone can define what is true and real. While his critics, judging from the platform of reflective thought, believe he is consciously lying, and liberal newspapers spent the first years of his presidency compiling compendious lists of his "lies," it is more likely that he actually believes each position he takes, regardless of its consistency, as his mind consists of a kaleidoscope of images rather than stable mental representations. What others differentiate as facts and consensual reality, even if perhaps they disagree with them, do not trouble him as he does not accept the existence of an external consensual reality different from what he, as a self-proclaimed genius, believes. Examples abound. He refused to accept the fact that he was soundly defeated in a fairly conducted presidential election, and insisted that malignant powers "stole" the election from him. When he realized the Constitution differed from what he believed, he said perhaps it should be revised. He not only refused to accept scientific findings about things like the COVID-19 virus and global warming, he asserted that he as a genius knew better. Further evidence of his inability to differentiate internal process from external consensual reality is the fact that the things he accuses others of are usually acts of criminality, deception, and hostility that more accurately describe behaviors of his that he either denies or believes are reasonable.

For example, Trump claimed that the marriage of political critic Elizabeth Warren was a "phony, disgusting deal" while dismissing as false significant evidence not only that he had numerous extra-marital affairs but that he has been repeatedly used his position of power to exploit and sexually abuse women and has boasted of his success being able to fondle their bodies at will.

During the 2016 election campaign, he did not content himself with disagreeing with his opponent Hillary Clinton; he portrayed her as evil and criminal. He was not being metaphorical; he literally called her a criminal and encouraged his followers at rallies to chant "jail her, lock her up" and pick fights with her supporters, reminiscent of lynch mob behavior. And he did everything he could to have her investigated for crimes there was no objective evidence she had committed. Some of the "crimes" he accused her of, related to Russia and to collusion with big business, were actually things there was abundant evidence he himself was guilty of but denied.

At a speech to Jews at the Israeli American Council on December 8, 2019, Trump, who regularly boasted what a wonderful man he is, despite well-documented behavior toward others in ruthless pursuit of the aggrandizement of his own real-estate empire, said "A lot of you are in the real estate business because I know you very well, you're brutal killers, not nice people at all."

A particularly striking example of his inability to recognize and respect others' separateness and right to differ with him is his contempt for the

32 The distinctive languages of each mental structure

tripartite system of government and the constitutional separation of powers. He has relentlessly attacked separation and independence of the legislative and judiciary branches of government and attempted to bring them under his control, and he has stated that if the Constitution does not agree with him it should be revised.

Trump is concrete and action oriented. He openly disparages science and its consensual reflective validation of knowledge. During the COVID-19 pandemic he dismissed scientific findings and recommendation with contempt, claimed that he is a genius who follows the truth that his "gut" tells him, and even advocated things like drinking bleach to kill the virus, at the same time that when he contracted the illness himself, he demanded and expected the best medicines available.

Hardly a day goes by without him calling people who he believes are different from him names and encouraging others to join in. While his intolerance of difference has been most visibly focused on color, and White supremacy, he does not hesitate viciously attacking anyone who disagrees with him. During the final apocalyptic destructive phase of his presidency when it was apparent that he had lost the election, Trump gave a speech to his followers in which he incited them to invade the Capitol, the literal and symbolic seat of government, assault the legislators within who were about to certify the Electoral College vote confirming his loss to Biden in the election, and kill the Vice President who had refused his command to falsify the election results. Here are some excerpts from his inflammatory speech to his followers on January 6, 2020. His confusion between self and other is evident, and not just oratorical:

> "**We will never give up**. We will never concede. It doesn't happen. You don't concede when there's theft involved. Our country has had enough. **We will not take it anymore, and that is what this is all about.** And to use a favorite term that all of you people really came up with, **we will stop the steal....** Republicans are constantly **fighting like a boxer with his hands tied behind his back**. It's like a boxer. And we want to be so nice. We want to be so respectful of everybody, including **bad people**. And we're going to have to **fight much harder**. We're going to walk down to the Capitol, and we're going to cheer on our brave senators and congressmen and women, and we're probably not going to be cheering so much for some of them, because you'll never take back our country with weakness. **You have to show strength**, and you have to be strong.

Former Vice President Mike Pence, and Nancy Pelosi, Senate majority leader, managed to escape the wrathful mob that sought them out accompanied by murderous chants; but less than a year later a demented follower broke into the Pelosi's San Francisco home in search of her, and beat her husband senseless with a hammer.

Trump's rambling oration to the January 6th mob is remarkable not only as an illustration of his destructiveness, but for the complete confusion and undifferentiation between self and other, subject and object, and about who is doing or is to do what to whom, that I turn to next. This same man told an audience at a political rally that he had been cheated of the Nobel Peace Prize!

Trump regularly mis-uses pronouns in the kinds of ways that are characteristic of infants who are as yet unable to differentiate self from others. At an award ceremony for Native Americans who served as code breakers in World War II, for example, he stated "We have a representative in Congress who they say was here a long time ago. They call her Pocahontas. But you know what, I like you." As it was Trump who used Pocahontas as a derogatory epithet for Elizabeth Warren we would expect to hear a subjective "I" to acknowledge his authorship, but instead he speaks as an undifferentiated "we" and "they." His concluding "I" is consistent with his failure to take ownership of the epithet demeaning Native Americans he used only seconds before. He regularly refers to the author of actions he has taken or intends to take by presidential decree as "we." And he frequently refers to "Donald Trump" as though he were someone else referring to him, the way mothers refer to their children early in development. For example, he tweeted that the "…Trump/Russia story was an excuse used by the Democrats as justification for losing the election. Perhaps Trump just ran a great campaign?"

The preceding illustrations that Trump's mind functions according to the primordial structure and its language, rather than in reflective representational thought, are only samples of the numerous areas of adult life, normal and abnormal, constructive and destructive, where they can be found. Throughout the book there will be others. A chapter is devoted to belief systems based on primordial mentation and language that underlie social systems that come into sometimes violent conflict with other social groupings based on reflective thought, including ones based on extreme ideologies, oppressive authoritarian governments, and cults. Another chapter describes individual psychopathology from the perspective that the classical psychoanalytic model of neurosis is predicated on a personality structure and language based for the most part on reflective thought, whereas the spectrum of psychosis is based on primordial structure. Turning to constructive manifestations, the behavior of good parents toward their infants was described. Creativity, the basis of some of the major cultural products of our civilization, is beyond the scope of the book, however.

5

THE STRUCTURE COMMON TO ALL SPECIES AND ITS MANIFESTATIONS

The primordial mental structure that is common to many species including humans can be inferred to have its human origins during the third trimester of gestation when REM changes, that in adults underlie most dreaming, are first observed on the fetal EEG (Schwab, Groh, Schwab, & Witte, 2009; Capellini, Preston, McNamara, Barton, & Nunn, 2009). At this time the auditory system also comes online. This is when learning from the environment, most particularly sounds and movements of mother, commences. REM sleep has been documented in terrestrial placental mammals and in birds, as well as in humans (Capellini, Preston, McNamara, Barton, & Nunn, 2009), providing inferential neurological evidence that primordial mental activity is not unique to humans. Anecdotal evidence from pet owners indicates that many people are convinced from observation that their dogs dream.

Maturation is sufficiently advanced at birth in some species, for example, turtles, that their instinctively programmed capacity to adapt and function independently in the limited environment where they will spend their lives is sufficiently developed that they do not need the auxiliary presence of caretakers. The primordial structure is present in its most rudimentary form at birth and does not undergo further maturation. Most species however, humans and other primates included, cannot survive much less mature without benefit of an initial period of dependency on caregivers, so that a limited amount of learned growth of the primordial structure occurs. Although it is only in homo sapiens that individual members become more sophisticated as a result of early learning during the stages of attachment and separation, and gradually begin to develop a second mental structure. This is because humans are by far the least mature of species at birth. The frontal lobes and myelination, on which thinking depend, develop slowly in humans over the course of the first

DOI: 10.4324/9781003435785-5

two decades of life (Paus et al., 1999). This chapter focusses on the primordial structure and its language in the attachment phase of human development and the next on the transition that occurs during the separation phase related to the acquisition of the second mental structure.

Our understanding of the psychological significance of the lengthy phases of attachment and separation unique to human beings, and their consequences for development of a second uniquely human mental structure and its language, owes much to the classic 1969 three-volume work of John Bowlby. Bowlby wrote that attachment communication between mother and infant includes "facial expression, posture, and tone of voice" (1969, p. 120). Two years later James and Joyce Robertson made a now classic film series demonstrating frame to frame synchronization of nuanced interactions between infants and their mothers, and their disruption and re-connection during separation and reunion. Since then, assisted by the development of sophisticated neuroscience technology such as fMRI that measures interactions directly at the neural level and can safely be applied to newborn infants, research into infant-mother attachment and the emergence of self and language has exploded. For an excellent overall summary of these developments see the 2014 book by Ammaniti and Gallese.

Prior to the third trimester of uterine life the fetus responds reflexively to stimulation. The embryonic sensory-perceptual-motor apparatus is sufficiently developed by the third trimester to activate the primordial mental system. The neurological foundation of learning in utero has already been mentioned, but there is evidence for its existence beyond speculation. The acquisition of knowledge prior to birth can be measured in newborn infants (Partanen & Virtala, 2017). One of the most powerful catalytic forces consists of the musical prosody of mother's voice as she talks to her unborn child as well as to others, using language and other forms of vocalization. The manifestations of quickening, or movement, in the later stages of pregnancy that are unrelated to maternal volition provide mothers-to-be with inescapable evidence that they harbor a new life, and motivate them to begin to interact with their fetuses with intentional and inadvertent vocalizations.

Darwin described the relationship between musicality, language, and attachment in 1871. Many others have written about it since. "The melodies of mother's speech are compelling auditory stimuli, which are particularly effective in eliciting emotion in pre-verbal infants" (Fernald, 1984, 1987). At birth, the infant has already learned to recognize the uniqueness of mother's voice and demonstrates by things like sucking response that baby prefers it to others (Kolata, 1984). In fact, newborn infants can distinguish mother's voice from a stranger's voice after hearing a single syllable in the first second of speech. Research has demonstrated that infants are born with preferences for things associated with the maternal voice that they learned prior to birth. Development of the language of primordial consciousness in utero includes

36 The structure common to all species and its manifestations

not only the learning of prosody but also of actual words and sentences within the self-other undifferentiated system of consciousness that prevails at that time. Kolata (1984) demonstrated that infants who were read Dr. Seuss's *The Cat in the Hat* twice a day, beginning in the last six weeks of gestation, sucked preferentially after birth when mother read that story in contrast to when she read a different Seuss story. Partanen et al. (2013) repeatedly exposed fetuses during the last trimester to particular combinations of nonsense syllables and discovered that subsequent to birth they recognized and preferentially responded to them in contrast to others. In the newborn, vision and kinesthesia join forces with these sensory modalities, along with the motor system, and these act in concert to create the mother-infant bond.

Although the maternal voice plays such an important role in human attachment via shared primordial mentation, it is not essential. Masataka (1996) studied a group of deaf mothers and their congenitally deaf infants and discovered unique qualities of motherese in sign language – slower tempo, exaggerated gesture, and more repetition – and demonstrated that the infants responded preferentially to a tape of their mothers signing material in motherese than when the same material was presented by other adults. I am not aware of any research on whether the fact that bonding in these deaf infants cannot begin until after birth has a particular effect on subsequent development.

The newborn human infant is adept at imitation or mirroring of what it sees. Trevarthen (1980) has demonstrated that only hours after birth infants are capable of sophisticated imitation of gestures and expressions of adults who interact with them.

First-time parents are often amazed, even shocked, to discover the seemingly reflexive facial expressions, high-pitched vocalizations, and unusual gestures with which they interact in a kind of mutually mirroring choreography with their infants; ways of being that are totally discrepant with how they interact with other adults. Mothers use language as though it were the infant speaking, mimicking its prosody and using the infant's name, or "we," and articulating what she imagines the infant to be thinking and feeling. The two speak together in a self-other undifferentiated affect-saturated action language. They are unwittingly employing the primordial mental structure and its language themselves. This language is colloquially called "baby talk" or "motherese" (Durkin, Rutter & Tucker, 1982; Fernald & Kuhl, 1987; Grieser & Kuhl, 1988) and reflects a primordial mental process qualitatively different from the reflective thought of adult life. This mother tongue is universal regardless of the particulars of specific languages, suggesting that its origins are biological, not learned. Ferguson (1964) documented its presence in six different language speaking countries. However, accented prosody enables the fetus and then the infant to differentiate the native tongue from similar content in other languages (Werker & Tees, 1984).

The structure common to all species and its manifestations **37**

Mother and infant initially function as a dual unity not only in mirroring interactions, but behaviorally, as mother serves necessary functions the infant is unable to perform. The infant exists in a mental state Margaret Mahler (1968) called omnipotence as it is unaware of dependency on a separate caregiver to perform essential life-sustaining functions. The implicit aim of good mothering is to keep the infant from having to experience utter, time-less, terrifying helplessness during the gradual process of assumption of inde-pendence and responsibility. The maternal functions are not differentiated from the actions and intentions of its own arms and legs. Infants will become upset and thrash about when a need or urge is experienced, and mother is not immediately present to assuage it. As the psychoanalyst D.W. Winnicott remarked (1951) from a psychological perspective, "there is no such thing as a baby." Reciprocally, the infant is unaware that there is any such thing as a mother, and it is not until well into the acquisition of the second mental structure, reflective thought, that it begins to learn that mother is a separate person. Werker and Tees (1984) observed that mothers speak to infants using the infant's name or "we" as though it were the infant speaking, mimic its prosody, and articulate what they intuit the infant is thinking and feeling. The two speak together in a self-other undifferentiated affect-saturated action language in which the mother initially provides the words that the infant eventually learns as its own.

Until sometime late in the second year of life infants do not use first per-son pronouns as there is no reflective awareness of a separate self. Names of objects are also used without awareness of separateness. Hence, they take a particular delight in naming, for it is initially equivalent to controlling the person or object, first experienced as a part of the self. Most parents intui-tively understand this and act instrumentally on their infant's behalf, fetching the named object if possible. Infants initially use their own given names as mother did, referring to themselves objectively not as "I" but by their given name. Second and third person pronouns, that in reflective thought denote otherness, are initially used in an undifferentiated way, for example, "we" rather than "I." Sayings like "sticks and stones will break my bones, but names will never hurt me" come from the period in which the child is learning that names are just thoughts, symbols, ideas. Most of us learn to recognize the dif-ference between the word and the object, to respect the differences of others so long as they are not directly trying to hurt us, to recognize the difference between our wishes and reality, and we come to express anger in discourse without throwing epithets as though they were things.

In this early undifferentiated phase of development, mothers typically and necessarily endow their infants with characteristics that become part of their identities as they grow. For example, the cries of Beng infants in West Africa are given meaning as expressions of the language of dead ancestors whose souls the babies are believed to embody. The Beng belief might seem similar

38 The structure common to all species and its manifestations

to some Western cultural beliefs that the infant embodies characteristics of deceased family members, but the Western instances are more complex as they combine the understanding of reflective thought with the belief of primordial mentation. Ashkenazi Jews, for example, imbue naming with a concrete sense of annihilation/reincarnation and believe one does not name a baby after a living ancestor; but most Jews would acknowledge that the baby is not, in fact, the ancestor.

During the first years of life the realms of reality and fantasy are interchangeable in play. Things like imaginary companions, the degree of certainty there may be monsters under the bed, and the extent to which small children get caught up in familiar children's tales, attest to this incomplete differentiation.

Until late in the second year of life the development of human infants and other primates is more or less similar. The mirror experiment devised by Gordon Gallup (1970, 1982) demonstrated that many animals other than humans also possess the ability to recognize themselves as objects and agents.

6

ACQUISITION OF THE SECOND MENTAL STRUCTURE DURING THE SEPARATION PHASE OF DEVELOPMENT

Compared to our most advanced primate relatives, chimps and bonobos, who reach sexual maturity and functional independence no later than six or seven years of age, humans require about two decades of functional dependence on caregivers. This post-partum immaturity is known as neoteny, and it is the biological foundation of the human difference. Its psychological consequences – dependency, and learning from caregivers (including development of the second mental structure unique to humans) – are the subject of this chapter.

Reflective thought gradually emerges from the undifferentiated mother-infant matrix if the attachment phase is good enough to enable the infant to begin the separation process that involves awareness of a self different from the world, the community and the caregivers; and the infant feels sufficiently secure to experience being separate, and in that sense alone in the world, with a mind of her own that is not always in accord with other minds. When maternal attachment is secure, the infant feels confident to explore the world beyond mother and to begin to think for herself.

The "second language" that adaptively supersedes but does not replace primordial mental activity begins to emerge between 1 ½ and 3 years of age, and under normal conditions the "baby talk" with mother gradually recedes into the social background (Johnson, & Newport,1989).

Self-reference in speech is one of the first indications of reflective representational thought (Sharpless, 1985). Use of the pronoun "I" begins to connote subjective awareness, and reciprocally the appropriate use of second and third person pronouns develops as recognition of the separateness of others and acquisition of social roles in conversation. The child begins to refer to his or her activities with a sense of possessiveness or ownership ("my" or "mine") that differentiates them from others, and to articulate associated inner

DOI: 10.4324/9781003435785-6

40 Acquisition of the second mental structure

affective states, marking the transition from the somatic affect characteristic of the primordial structure to the beginning of specific emotional awareness. Whereas hitherto the child talked mostly about the environment, labeling objects and their qualities and describing activities, now she begins to comment on her own activities, reflecting on what she has done, demonstrating rudimentary representational memory and emotional awareness. The transition from the primordial conscious language of agency and doing in the world, to the language of awareness of the differentiated self and other is manifest by the "show and tell" that is such an important aspect of early development. Labeling of one's body parts also begins around this time, also signifying self-awareness that encompasses body ownership. Mother and child play body-part naming games. Sayings like "sticks and stones will break my bones, but names will never hurt me" arise during this period of gradual recognition that names are just thoughts and do not possess the concrete force of physical actions. Most of us grow beyond exclusive use of primordial mentation and learn to respect others, recognize the difference between our wishes and reality, and come to express anger in emotional statements without throwing epithets or engaging in destructive actions. Some do not. Adjectival name-calling often based on bodily activities and products that has the feeling of hitting and being hit is far more extensive in those who have not made the secure transition from the primordial structure to reflective symbolic thought.

Stable use of personal pronouns and given names to distinguish reflective self from separate others, along with such developments as the ability to say "no" (and later "yes"), and to enter and leave the world of primordial mental make-believe volitionally, is a gradual process. With this stability and security, the child can begin to function in a world in which the separateness of others on whom she depends is recognized, along with the possibility that they will frustrate her desires by doing things she does not like and the ability to sustain self-esteem and respect for the separateness of the other in such situations.

In normal development, in Western culture, ages five to seven appear to mark a developmental watershed. It is no longer possible to learn a second language with the prosody or accent of the mother tongue, suggesting that the learning that occurs is no longer based upon primordial mentation (Rivera-Gaxiola, Silvia-Pereyra, & Kuhl, 2005). In many cultures, it is around this age that the first concrete separation from the family via formal education commences, probably because the average child possesses sufficient reflective thought capacity to consciously strive to learn and acquire representational remembered knowledge from the environment. Education changes from methods primarily related to fantasy, play, and group activities, all based on primordial mentation, and becomes focused on individual reflective learning: the "three R's," in which the child is required to distinguish the worlds of fantasy from consensual reality as articulated by teachers and codified in books; and required to adaptively distinguish between the mental process appropriate to classroom learning and that appropriate to recess, where resumption of primordial mentation and fantasy play are encouraged. Humans, and by extension homo sapiens, are no longer stimulus-bound, and like the fictional gorilla in the Kubrick movie *2001* can make the soaring transition to creative thought.

This is not a transition all children are able to make; and some not even in part, although the continued acquisition of formal language that is common to both mental processes may effectively masquerade this fact and enable some to acquire a false self. It is important to realize that in normal development the capacity for and use of primordial conscious mentation and its language persists in ways that are adaptive; it simply becomes regulated by self-awareness of what is and is not socially appropriate and useful in a given context. When this transition cannot be made, in whole or in part, problems related to the primordial structure that are maladaptive and destructive arise.

In the process of development, infants need to learn to identify and control painful emotions such as fear, rage, shame and guilt, as well as love and other caring emotions. This involves a process of identifying and representing many somatic-affective sensations as well as amorphous affects, such as anxiety and depression, with appropriate emotions and their concomitant ideation, differentiated with regard to self and other.

Caring for her infant's mind and helpless body is a remarkable and difficult challenge for even the most mature mother. Mothers who have not securely acquired a second mental structure because their own infancy had been insecure and chaotic cannot make a stable realistic distinction between their infants' needs and their own, and the dysphoric affects associated with the sense of deprivation. They tend to perceive their infants as hostile, threatening beings. Starting with the first signs of fetal movement such mothers begin to "talk" to their infants in negative, threatening ways, much of it in privacy where no one else can hear.

In 1949, Winnicott listed 18 reasons for a mother to hate her infant, and the aggression and destructiveness that their infants may display in response. Mary Ainsworth (1978, 1982), a student of John Bowlby, devised a way to study some of his propositions about healthy and pathological attachment and separation, exposing 12–18-month-old infants and their mothers to what she called the "strange situation" experiment. It consisted of one-way screen observation of infants with and without their mothers and with a stranger, in a variety of combinations. She classified infant attachment behavior into four affect-driven categories. Affects were defined as psychosomatic experiences like crying and thrashing that antedate the ability to articulate specific emotions and their ideational contexts such as "I'm angry…or frightened… or despairing…or panicked…because…." In other words, affects are experienced in lieu of thoughts in which emotions and related ideas are represented and can be reflected on. Ainsworth's classifications are consistent with the

42 Acquisition of the second mental structure

hypothesis that infants function according to the characteristics of primordial consciousness mentation.

She observed three kinds of infant behavior: secure, ambivalent-resistant, and anxious-avoidant. Secure infants were able to begin to separate, as manifest by making the transition between relating to mother and exploring the environment, and in the stranger situation were able to do some exploration without showing undue distress.

Ambivalent-resistant infants were anxious and passive at home and preoccupied with mother and her whereabouts in the laboratory. Mothers of ambivalent-resistant infants were observed to be insensitive to their infant's needs and unpredictable in their responses but were not overtly rejecting.

Anxious-avoidant infants were intolerant of separations and tended to be anxious and act as though they were angry; their mothers were rejecting of them. Although they could not separate from her, in mother's presence the infants tended to ignore her and treat her as though she was not present.

Another category of infant behavior, disorganized-disoriented, was conceptualized by Ainsworth's student and collaborator, Mary Main (1977, 1982). These infants were anxious, disorganized, and confused; their behavior was often disruptive. They seemed caught in oscillations between approach and avoidance. Their mothers were characterized by the observer as frightening and unpredictable and showed no signs of consistent attachment to their babies. Mary Main comments on one peculiarity of the language of these infants that seems relevant to primordial consciousness, namely the presence of contradictions in their speech.

Lyons-Ruth (2003) and the Boston Change Process Study Group (BCPSG; 2007) formulated their own model of disorganized attachment. They tested infants of caregivers who behaved in ways that were rejecting and attacking and distorted the meaning of infant initiatives by responding to them with dissonant or inappropriate affects. When exposed to new learning situations with others, infants of such mothers manifested the kind of maladaptive and self-destructive responses (for instance, confusion, mistrust and hostility) that observers interpreted as paranoid, but might have been adaptive responses to the rejection, attack, and confusion consequent to their mothers' behavior. Nascent efforts on the part of such infants to represent and articulate emotions of fear and rage were ignored, rejected, or attacked by their mothers.

Infants who have not had a stable, secure, attentive attachment experience not only fail to develop a second mental structure based on an integrated internally consistent sense of themselves, but their subjective world also consists of the dysphoric somatic-affective precursors of rage, fear, despair, and insecurity, experienced in primordial structural terms that do not distinguish what is going on in the world from their own intrapsychic state. Such reactions are dramatized in action, and to an observer might seem paranoid, delusional, and mistrustful.

Acquisition of the second mental structure 43

The children of such disturbed mothers are unable to make the normal adaptive transition from the primordial structure to predominant selective use of the second structure of reflective representational thought that is necessary for separation from mother. Instead, they perceive others as figments of their own dangerous imaginations and sometimes tend to gravitate toward more destructive people because they are more familiar. Use of the primordial structure persists in situations where it is not contextually appropriate because the sense of self and world has been so severely traumatized and distorted. Moreover, actual efforts to separate, for example, to start school and form relationships with friends and eventually with intimates, subject the child to a state of awareness of helpless dependency in a world that is not experienced realistically, but is perceived as frightening and dangerous because it is animated with hostile qualities from the child's own undifferentiated unintegrated mind.

The state of separateness is literally unthinkable for such children. Remaining in the unseparated, undifferentiated mental state of primordial consciousness becomes an adaptive solution; a kind of false security that depends upon not knowing and having to struggle with intolerably painful emotions.

In Chapter 4, former President Donald Trump was used as an example of an adult whose mental functioning appears to be based on the primordial mental structure rather than on reflective representational thought. Material about Trump's childhood that might help us understand his apparent developmental difficulties during the attachment-separation phase of infant development that seems to have eventuated in his inability to acquire a second mental structure. He is closed about his childhood as with all details of his personal life other than occasional expressions of admiration for his father and a kind of pride in the evolution of their relationship from one of hostility and defiance to one in which he came to act much like father and got father's support for doing so. He has little to say about his mother or the rest of the family. Whether his reluctance is a conscious expression of secrecy, which would imply his mind does differentiate the passage of time and he wishes to hide his origins in order to protect his image; or whether, more consistent with primordial mental function, he enacts elements of the past rather than being able to remember and reflect on them is not clear. He has used legal means along with his enormous wealth to extract non-disclosure agreements from women including his first wife and suppress whatever information about him they might have. Until recently the 2015 history of the Trump dynasty by Gwenda Blair, sparse on Trump's life as it is, and lacking in information about how she documented what she wrote, has been the most complete source of information. In 2020, his niece Mary Trump published a more detailed account, in defiance of one of his numerous non-disclosure agreements, and despite legal attempts of Trump and other family members to block publication.

44 Acquisition of the second mental structure

Most of what follows comes from her biography, which is consistent with what little was previously known.

Although niece Mary is a clinical psychologist with an excellent reputation, it must be noted that she is hardly an unbiased objective biographer. Mary obviously dislikes her uncle, and much of what she writes about Trump's childhood probably came from her father Fred Jr., Trump's older brother. He had reason for animosity as he was openly denigrated and mistreated by their father Fred Sr. and by Donald. Fred Jr. was the only sibling who tried to separate himself from the undifferentiated family identity and literally fly the coop (he became an airline pilot). His effort aborted tragically, with death from alcoholism at age 42. However, to balance the scales of justice somewhat, Mary's effort to separate from the family has involved trying to understand it and has led to her becoming a respected clinical psychologist.

Trump's mother Mary was the youngest of ten children. She came to the United States at age 18, from the Scottish Hebrides, now the site of one of his golf courses whose importance Trump regularly brags about. She became a domestic in the mansion of Andrew Carnegie in New York, where at age 24 she met her future husband, Fred Sr., then a rising financial magnate.

Trump's mother is descried by Trump's niece as a self-centered unpredictable woman who tried to use her children to feel good and was largely unaware of and attentive to their needs as separate persons. This fits Mary Ainsworth's (1982) description in Chapter 13 of rejecting mothers and their anxious-avoidant infants.

Mary had five children, two girls and three boys, of whom Donald was number four. Maryanne, the eldest sibling, is almost nine years older than Donald. Fred Jr., the next oldest, was 7 ½ years older than Donald. There was a 4 ½ year hiatus between Elizabeth, the second sister, and Donald. Mary was advised by her doctors not to have more children after Donald, but when he was around 1 ½ years of age, presumably at the height of the attachment-separation phase, mother became pregnant with her last child, Trump's younger brother Robert. Robert was born when Donald was two years and two months of age. About nine months after Robert's birth, when Donald would have been less than three, mother suffered a sudden life-threatening hemorrhage that required emergency hysterectomy and ovariectomy. Her life hung in the balance for a time and what mothering Donald had experienced seems to have vanished thereafter. In the year that followed, mother developed septicemia and required several additional surgeries. She developed severe osteoporosis as a consequence of removal of her ovaries. She was apparently accident-prone, and had frequent fractures as a result of the osteoporosis she acquired. She developed insomnia and nocturnal wandering as well; a characteristic Donald Trump also displays. Donald's care subsequent to her illnesses seems to have been divided between maids and his sister Maryanne, who was 12 at the time mother was hospitalized.

Information about father Fred, about whom more is known, has been saved for last, although his in-your-face hostility, much like that of his son, overshadows mother's much less conspicuous but probably more profound influence. The basic damage to Donald was almost certainly done before father administered the *coup de grace*. Father seems to have been a self-centered liar; an uncaring, sexist male who was verbally abusive to others including his children and was expert at manipulating others in order to get what he wanted, without regard to truth or scruples. He was an autocrat at home but was basically absent and preoccupied with his astronomically successful real estate career. Father was contemptuous of Donald's older brother Fred and encouraged Donald to join in ridiculing him. The failure to appreciate the separateness of others and requirement that others be clones of oneself is another characteristic shared by father and son. Donald's growing nasty defiant behavior presented a problem for father. Both within the family and at school Donald soon became out of control and socially incorrigible.

By the time Donald was 12 his elder brother Fred Jr. had labeled him "the great I am," an eerie echo of Trump's more recent statement that he is "a stable genius." Donald had become like father and acted contemptuous of outside authority. By age 13 no one could control him. Donald openly defied his mother, bullied his younger brother, was contemptuous of his older one, and was rebellious and out of control at school. Finally, father, who was on the school board, acceded to suggestions of others, and had him sent to a military boarding school.

The rest, as they say, is history. It is remarkable how Trump has been able to use his mind and behavior to compensate for deficits in his early upbringing, for example, by using his power to control women; even boasting about his success publicly manipulating women's bodies whenever he chooses. He has managed to become the center of everyone's attention and actualize his delusional belief that he is the greatest at everything he undertakes. Only two weeks after revealing he had what apparently was a severe case of COVID-19 and required an extraordinary combination of drugs in order to survive, he dismissed the severity of his illness and claimed that he felt "like Superman." Once at the mercy of the leaders of the military school to which he was sent as an adolescent, and presumably disciplined by its military leaders, as president he has not only demonstrated his reverence for the military, in his role as Commander-in-Chief he stocked his administration with high-ranking military, and though the relationships began as glowing honeymoons, once his picks showed evidence of having minds of their own, he capriciously turned on most of them and fired them.

7

LIMITATION OF THE BIOLOGICAL THEORY OF EVOLUTION IN UNDERSTANDING THE ORIGINS OF THE SECOND MENTAL STRUCTURE

It is important to understand what the generally accepted biological theory of evolution accounts for and what its limitations are in order to situate discussion of the origins of the second mental structure that is unique to human beings in an appropriate causal context.

The term "species" and the concept of evolution have become so deeply imbedded in common language use that most of us believe, without pausing to think about it, that we understand the meaning of these fundamental concepts. For that reason, I interrupt the continuity of the narrative to review basic history of the science of evolution.

Classification of species

As is true with many important ideas that appear to arise simultaneously from many sources, it is an oversimplification to attribute the origin of the study of diversity of living things to a single person. However, the work of the Swedish botanist Carl Linnaeus is a useful place to begin. Two hundred and fifty years ago, Linnaeus proposed the classification taxonomy of living things that is still used today. Though others less known preceded him, a century later Charles Darwin turned the spotlight on the concepts of species and of evolution. The work of these two has generated much heat along with light, and in an effort to clarify it in the century and a half since Darwin's work a new scientific discipline known as systematics has arisen to study the nature of biological diversity.

In 1735, during the age of enlightenment, Linnaeus proposed an elaborate seven-level descriptive classification system that is still widely used, beginning with the most general distinctions and working down layer by layer to specifics. The distinction between human beings and other primates is made

DOI: 10.4324/9781003435785-7

at level six, at which point the family of hominids is divided into four genera: pongo (orangutan), gorilla, pan, and homo (us). Some of these genera are further divided into species. The genus pan is divided into pan paniscus (the bonobo) and pan troglodyte (the chimpanzee). Of the genus homo, only sapiens exists today; Neanderthals are extinct, and erectus is presumed to be our ancestor. The members of genus homo were distinguished by large cranial capacity, erect posture and bipedal gait, opposable thumbs, and the ability to make sophisticated standardized tools.

Some consider Jean-Baptiste (Antoine Pierre) de Monet, the Chevalier de Lamarck, to be responsible for the study of evolution of species. In 1809, almost half a century before Darwin, he wrote *Philosophie Zoologique*, a treatise in which he coined the term *biology* and proposed the first scientific theory of evolution: all species are descendants of common simple forms. He encountered fierce criticism, however, including from Darwin half a century later, who called his ideas "nonsense" while ironically incorporating the idea of species descent into his own theory. In 1902, the German biologist Ernest Haeckel distinguished between the common descent aspect of evolution which he attributed to Lamarck and the natural selection aspect which he attributed to Darwin. Lamarck's belief that acquired characteristics could be transmitted has been ridiculed, but apparently his ideas were misunderstood because of poor translation of his books. The idea that the transmission is direct, and that the characteristics in question might be ones developed by use during life, is often ridiculed by illustration with the example that giraffes grow longer necks by exercise in order to get the choicest food, or the strength of the blacksmith might be inherited. He actually wrote: "For, whatever the environment may do, it does not invoke any direct modification in the shape and organization of animals."

Although Lamarck is usually misunderstood and dismissed out of hand, his ideas were re-activated in 1957 by the embryologist Conrad Waddington in the form of what he calls epigenetics. Epigenetics designates the complex of developmental processes between the genotype and phenotype; what is called the epigenome. He maintained that our life habits and experiences modify genetic material, and do not just contribute to the survival of organisms and selective propagation of their genes. Critics of epigenetics point out that the kinds of changes that are referred to consist of environmental and behavioral habit factors that tend to degrade the organism, hence the genetic changes, if any, would not be adaptive and would probably lead to species deterioration rather than to increasing the odds for species survival. That critique would certainly seem to apply to the aspect of destructiveness that seems unique to humans, except that, as we shall examine in the next chapter, the root cause of the life changes that are described is not the experiences themselves, but neoteny, the biological difference between humans and other species that makes the changes possible.

48 Limitation of the biological theory of evolution

A century after Linnaeus, in 1859, Darwin wrote *On the Origin of Species*. The hierarchical concept of evolution through natural selection is credited to him, although it was apparently discovered more or less concurrently and independently by Alfred Russel Wallace. The theory is that survival and transmission of the most adaptive mutations accounts for why species differ from one another and how they develop or evolve from common ancestry. Remarkably, Darwin never clearly defined what constitutes a species. He distinguished two groups of living things, species and varieties. In *Origin* he makes the somewhat ambiguous distinction:

> Hereafter we shall be compelled to acknowledge that the only distinction between species and well-marked varieties is, that the latter are known, or believed, to be connected at the present day [to existing species] by intermediate gradations, whereas species were formerly thus connected.
>
> *(1859, p. 485, bracketed comment mine)*

In *The Descent of Man* (1871) he writes:

> Practically, when a naturalist can unite two forms together by others having intermediate characters, he treats the one as a variety of the other, ranking the most common, but sometimes the one first described, as the species, and the other as the variety. But cases of great difficulty sometimes occur in deciding whether or not to rank one form as a variety of another, even when they are closely connected by intermediate links; nor will the commonly assumed hybrid nature of the intermediate links always remove the difficulty.
>
> *(pp. 214–215)*

He appears to be stating that species lack the obvious progression that would be suggested by intermediate forms, that he called varieties, even though they presumably evolved from varieties. By this criterion sapiens and neanderthal are varieties of genus homo, but only sapiens has survived as a species.

That Darwin's hypothesis of evolution by natural biological selection applied to humans as well is made clear in Chapter 6 of *Descent* when he states his belief that the mental differences that distinguish humans from other animals have unequivocal survival value. As we shall see, this was a dubious claim.

Early objections to Darwin's theory came from creationists; those who came to science through a Christian religious background and who were torn between scientific objectification and the Biblical teaching that humans are made by God in his image and hence are qualitatively different from and superior to savage animal creatures. Richard Owens (1860) proposed a quasi-religious definition of species that continues to have supporters today, based on breeding purity. In other words, if two animals could not mate and produce young then they were of different species. By this criterion, chimps and

Limitation of the biological theory of evolution **49**

humans are not members of the same species. Darwin disagreed with the proposition that hybrid sterility is an adequate definition of speciation. What these critics failed to take into account is that the human species is different from others, but the difference is fundamentally caused by a biological difference (neoteny); using religious beliefs to account for it is misguided.

Ernst Mayr and Theodosius Dobzhansky, two of the most influential of twentieth-century contributors to the field of systematics, also objected to Darwin's theory that species are continuous with lower-level forms and have evolved by natural selection based on survival. They proposed instead that species are populations that have become reproductively inbred because of geographic isolation from one another.

Gregor Mendel's nineteenth-century discovery of genetics through his research with plants, propelled by subsequent advances in biology and the development of sophisticated mathematical models, fundamentally altered the dialogue about species and directed the focus of the study of evolution toward understanding microscopic forms, genes and DNA. In the last century, distinct fields including population genetics, evolutionary biology, epigenetics, and molecular genetics have arisen along with efforts to integrate them. They share a common view of evolution based on biology and propagation of the genes whose phenotypes have proven most adaptive and have had lively debates over such things as the relative importance of genetic drift, gradual changes in a population related to the random disappearance of particular genes, and alteration of genes based on life experience that has led to selective propagation of their phenotypes.

Richard Dawkins (1976) wrote that genes, not species, are the evolving and surviving living structures; and described how they act indirectly, through their phenotypes or somatic embodiments. In his bestselling book *The Selfish Gene*, he described how natural selection modifies genes by favoring the survival and propagation of some phenotypes and not others. As Herbert Gintis (2011) points out, transmission via selection of phenotypes is epigenetic, not genetic. That is, it is the study of the expression of genes, not the genes themselves.

In efforts to relate the microscopic world of molecular genetics to the macroscopic world of living animals, the Smithsonian Human Evolution Project has studied the genetic similarities and differences among members of the genera pan and homo. The variation in DNA among humans is but 0.1 percent. Between humans on the one hand, and chimps and bonobos on the other, it is just 1.2 percent. The difference between chimps, bonobos, and humans considered as a group, and gorillas, is 1.6 percent. In other words, there is a 98.5 percent similarity in DNA amongst us. DNA, however, is a building block, and it can be present in different quantities and different configurations in the genome. When complexities such as this are taken into account there appears to be a 4–5 percent difference between humans and chimpanzees.

8

EFFORTS TO FIT WHAT MAKES HUMANS UNIQUE INTO THE BIOLOGICAL THEORY OF EVOLUTION LEAD TO THE NEED FOR A REVISION

In 1895 James Baldwin, a Princeton psychologist, expressed his concern that a theory of evolution based exclusively on biological inheritance does not take into account the evolutionary role of the complex thinking, civilization, and social sophistication that distinguish humans from other species. Donald Campbell (Hayes & Hull 2001), originator of what is known as realistic conflict theory, continued the discussion. Despite some of the modifications that ensued, summarized in the chapter, no theory of evolution provides an adequate explanation of human culture and civilization; or of the unique extent, depth, and virulence of human destructiveness, because they all come back to biology as the root cause of change.

For example, Joseph Henrich (2015) proposes that cultural evolution makes humans unique, and that its defining characteristic is social: the capacity to learn from one another. He operates within a classical Darwinian framework insofar as he believes cultural learning is transmitted through genetic perpetuation of an adaptive phenotype. It is difficult to imagine, however, how the exceptional destructiveness characteristic of humans might be a phenotype that favors survival.

A few theorists recognize that an adequate theory of evolution must make some reference to the uniqueness of human destructiveness as well as civilized "progress." In his 1992 book *Sick Societies,* Robert Edgerton attempts to dispel the myth of the noble savage and the associated idealized myth of our pre-civilized ancestors. However, he does not elaborate the evolutionary significance of his observation.

Richerson and Boyd (2006) describe what they called the theory of gene-culture coevolution, or dual inheritance theory. It proposes that the biological and the social-cultural comprise a complex system with emergent properties.

DOI: 10.4324/9781003435785-8

They give such examples as the evolution of the human brain and vocal apparatus, changes that in turn enable social communication and learning and therefore create phenotypes that in their opinion favor survival, and hence are selectively transmitted and perpetuated. However, social communication and human learning have been used for destructive as well as constructive purposes and therefore are not clearly survival-adaptive. The authors do recognize human destructiveness, but they share E. O. Wilson's sociobiological beliefs that it is a constructive social regulatory mechanism and when it goes overboard it is a statistically insignificant aberration: when we aim for a target, a few times we will miss the mark.

Robert Paul (2015) believes that learned knowledge and the civilization and culture that it has produced, and basic biology are independent entities, and that humans are biologically aggressive and destructive. The genetic element, in his view, is the male imperative to reproduce, which leads to violence and destructiveness. The evolution of this apparent human difference from other species is not made clear. Human culture controls the violence and emphasizes community and cooperation. Culture progressively triumphs, and accounts for what Paul considers the success of our species. It is mediated through symbol and language. He believes, as did Wilson, that humans are a socially superior, altruistic, cooperative species that are destined to continue to successfully solve the problems that arise, including those that are destructive.

Paul does not deal with the evolutionary origins of the human difference, destructiveness, and civilization. And he equates civilization and the presumed superiority of our species with the capacity for language and symbolism. However, symbolism, and more broadly language itself, can be used for destructive as well as constructive purposes. Words such as black and white, republican and democrat, socialist, vaccine, gun, police, even Nazi, can be used in ways that are culturally constructive or destructive depending on user and context.

David Graeber (Graeber & Wengrow, 2021) and Elizabeth Kolbert (2014, 2021) write about the destructive aspect of the human difference from a popular non-academic perspective. The late anthropologist David Graeber was a politically active anarchist, whose extreme views appear to have played a part in Yale's refusal to renew his contract as associate professor. The reason I mention this is that it is suggestive evidence that his theory is not separate and distinct from his political beliefs. He claims that the proposition that we have evolved from savage destructive ancestry to increasingly complex forms of social organization, many of which are destructive, is incorrect. From his anarchistic perspective, he believes humans have always had the freedom to choose between more or less repressive forms of governance, and that these options have spawned the variety of social organizations throughout history, some more destructive than others. Because Graeber does not understand that

52 Revision of the biological theory of evolution

freedom to choose is the product of reflective thought – a structure unique to humans that has developed slowly over millennia and is still only used by some humans – and that reflective thought itself has had destructive as well as constructive consequences, he ignores basic questions related to the human difference and its evolution.

Elizabeth Kolbert writes about what she calls the sixth mass extinction in two books (2014, 2021). She attributes it to human beings, unlike the preceding five, but does not ask how and why humans have evolved so differently from other species.

Most of the optimistic social Darwinist views of human evolution have come from books designed to appeal to an audience that might prefer entertainment to unpleasant facts. Hence the great popular appeal of books by Steven Pinker and Uval Noah Harari. At a superficial level they support E. O. Wilson's late life thesis that humans are a eusocial species, like ants, but they do not reach that conclusion through careful scholarship. Steven Pinker's book *Enlightenment Now* (2018) views human nature through rose-colored glasses, blind to evidence of human destructiveness. He believes that as the result of stronger governments, education, cooperation among nations, increased prosperity, and increasing rights for women and minorities; war and violence are steadily declining and may eventually become obsolete so that presumably we will live happily and prosperously forever.

Uval Noah Harari is another contemporary apostle of the doctrine of social Darwinism. Harari's book *Sapiens* (2018) has gained great popularity with his thesis that advances in genetics and technology are leading inevitably to an ever more successful species, which will evolve in a humanoid or techno-human direction and presumably survive forever.

In the latter part of his career E. O. Wilson turned from the detailed study of insects and other non-human species to reflection about human social organization. The product is speculative, lacking the meticulous hands-on observational rigor characteristic of his field work with insects. It is worthy of mention both because of his stature in sociobiology, the discipline he originated, and insofar as it echoes the unrealistic social Darwinist optimism of the ideas just mentioned. It should in no way detract from the importance of his earlier work on species social organization in relation to species survival. In *The Social Conquest of Earth* (2012), he introduced the idea that human society is governed by what he called eusocial behavior. His hypothesis was modelled after the organization of ants, a species he considered an example of social success because of their ability not only to survive but to thrive under a remarkable variety of conditions. According to Wilson, a successful or eusocial species is one in which the members have transcended individual selfishness and self-aggrandizement, and divide and share the task of population survival and growth among themselves so that not only the survival of a species, but its expansion, is more important than that of any of its individual members. Wilson refers to eusocial species as "hive-minded super-cooperators."

Wilson overlooks the uniqueness of human destructiveness and some rather glaring differences between ant and human societies, in what appears to be wishful theorizing that humans are super-ants. He interprets population expansion as indicative of species success. However, in so doing he ignores critical differences such as size and species effects on planetary resources. Ants function as tillers of soil, scavengers of waste and vehicles for dispersing seeds and spreading vegetation, important ecological functions, whereas humans manufacture waste and destroy plant and animal species in the process of tilling the soil. Further, the growth of human population is having effects on social conflict and planetary resources of a nature and scale that bears no resemblance to the expansion of ant colonies. In 2002 Wilson himself estimated that if current rates of human-caused destruction of the biosphere continue, half of all extant species will be extinct by the turn of the next century. He never made comments remotely resembling this about ants!

None of these theories takes full cognizance of the human difference – two distinct mental structures that govern us in complex ways – and none makes a convincing case including both biology and psychology in its evolution. There is another biological difference, however, that has had enabling effects on human evolution and that explains how what makes humans unique relates to immaturity and complex learning. Several times earlier in the book I referred to what biologists call neoteny, the extended post-natal period of immaturity that has a unique effect on human development and species evolution. The consequences of neoteny are a prolonged enforced dependency on caregivers that enables and requires social learning and the acquisition of sophisticated knowledge, including development of a second mental structure, reflective representational thought. As a result, extensive learning occurs in the process of each individual person's development, and this learning leads to knowledge that becomes part of shared social-cultural knowledge, which can be transmitted and expanded from generation to generation. In other words, the theory of learning needs to be modified to include the fact that complex learned knowledge can function independently of biology as an evolutionary force. The content of this knowledge includes not only those elements that we consider civilized, creative, and culturally sophisticated, but also the attributes that make humans uniquely destructive.

The forces of change that stem from learning and the acquisition, accumulation, and intergenerational transmission of knowledge, have given rise to culture and civilization; but also, to an extent, intensity and virulence of human destructiveness that has no parallel among other species and is not easily accounted for by a biological reductive survival-adaptive theory of evolution. The theory of evolution needs to be revised to include the proposition that while the learning that has led to the second mental structure that makes humans unique is dependent on biology for its origin, it functions as an independent evolutionary force.

What are the evolutionary implications of human civilization and the complex interplay of constructive and destructive forces that comprise the human difference? There seem to be two possible consequences for the human species, one more optimistic than the other. The first is that however remarkable the difference between us and other primates may seem, the human species still conforms to the principles that govern life and death of other species that Wilson outlined in his first and most scientifically sound model of sociobiology, in which destructiveness serves a social regulatory function. This possibility poses major problems for humans who value individual life and yet have serious concerns about the future of our species and our planet. We humans would need to take drastic measures, some of which would be basically at odds with prevailing values and mores, if our species is to have a chance to survive. These problems are explored in the concluding chapters.

A second possibility is that the human difference fits neatly into the biological theory of evolution of species and homo sapiens as an instance of a fatal mutation or combination of mutations. In that case, neoteny and its consequences will not be compatible with long-term species survival. Considering the vast expanse of evolutionary time compared with the brief period that homo sapiens has walked the earth, perhaps our species is but a brief candle, an evolutionary mistake.

The manifestations of culture, civilization, and destructiveness and their complex interplay that have arisen as a result of the second mental structure, the fact that not all humans are able to traverse the attachment-separation phase of development with sufficient success to master its use, and the interactions between the two structures are the subject of a companion volume, *The Human Difference: Evolution, Civilization – and Destruction* (Robbins, in press).

9

THE ORIGINS OF SOCIAL STRUCTURE FROM MENTAL STRUCTURE

The social organization derived from the primordial structure

When homo sapiens commenced the process of separation from our primate ancestors, social organization must have been based on the primordial structure in which the person was not a separate individual but served as a cog in the social system whose function was survival and maintenance of group homeostasis, without regard for the fate of individual members. Notions of intellectual growth and creativity beyond immediate circumstantial survival, and acquisition of new horizons of knowledge, were yet to come as part of the evolution of a second mental structure, reflective thought, and the social groupings that would emerge from it. The social organizations that evolved from the emergence of a second mental structure have not replaced the primordial structure and its function that we share with other animals, including our primate ancestors, or supplanted all social groupings based on the primordial structure; human society just became more complex. The primordial structure continues to function normally in such things as individual parenting and creativity, and social groupings organized around constructive belief systems; and pathologically in maladaptive persistence of the primordial structure in individuals and organizations based on malignant ideologies, as well as inevitable social clashes between groups.

The best analysis of the social nature of species other than homo sapiens, and by inference, human society at the dawn of homo sapiens, evolution, is that of E. O. Wilson, creator of the field known as sociobiology. In his groundbreaking study of animal societies, *A New Synthesis* (1975), Wilson describes how, what from our contemporary perspective appears to be individual destructiveness, is responsible for homeostasis and survival of species in most animal societies. He describes two types of genetically based population control mechanisms, R and K.

DOI: 10.4324/9781003435785-9

56 Origins of social structure from mental structure

R behaviors are ones in which individual members of a group appear to sacrifice their lives for the greater good of the community. Their individual destruction serves a larger function of helping to increase a population whose numbers are dwindling. There are numerous examples of R behavior in non-human species and some, but far fewer, in humans.

Wilson's other category, K, or kin selection, is characterized by acts of aggression and destruction toward others of one's species that tend to reduce the size of an overcrowded group and refine the survival quality of the surviving members. It is what is known colloquially as "survival of the fittest," and involves competition for scarce resources. The resources in question may be territorial including nesting, food, and other limited supplies, the most desirable females, or tribal dominance. Dominance in males involves propagation, hence control of females, and dominance in females involves competition for males and control over child-bearing and rearing. While the consequences of both mechanisms are destructive to some individual members, they serve to stabilize and perpetuate the social group in relation to available resources.

For all species that are not fully mature and independent at birth the family, or what substitutes for it, is the first group. Our first experience of social organization consists of childhood immersion in whatever system provides us with life-sustaining food, shelter, and a modicum of purposeful organization. As with other species, the group experience is shaped by the primordial structure with which we are born. As a result of uniquely human evolution and variety of individual development consequent to its complexity, unlike the situation in other species whose organization is largely biologically determined, human infants and children have no guarantee they will be nurtured in a caring nuclear family or even have a single caring parent. This initial organization, in all its vicissitudes, serves as a mental template for formation and membership in the larger social organizations that are a part of adult life. Whether the first group supports individual development beyond the primordial structure and acquisition of the second structure varies, and it is the resultant structural variety among individuals that determines the variety and complexity of human social organizations.

One remarkable difference between the human species and other animals, including our primate ancestors, is that most other species rear their young in intact biologically programmed family structures typical for the species. This is because their social structure is exclusively built upon the primordial mental structure. The human family, by contrast, is significantly impacted by the second mental structure, reflective thought, as well, and its vicissitudes are based upon the individual and social differences in parenting and child-rearing related to idiosyncratic learning experiences that parents had as children. The family – or whatever has come to substitute for it due to the vicissitudes of human learning – is our first experience in a social group, and the experience comes at a time when infants and small children cannot differentiate themselves from others and from the world, and the elements of proto-self that are not differentiated have yet to be integrated into a separate individual sense of self. In other words, the original group, experienced via the primordial mental structure, is a shared belief system.

One of the most profound thinkers about the nature of groups was Wilfred Bion (*Experiences in Groups, 1961*). He writes that the primordial mental organization that characterizes groups "is one in which physical and psychological are as yet undifferentiated" (1951, p. 103).

To supplement the analysis of E. O. Wilson based on his study of other species there is inferential evidence from existing human tribes to suggest that the original human social groups were much like those of other animals. Despite hundreds of years of colonization by civilizations based on reflective representational thought, some tribal cultures have remained relatively pristine and resistant to change. From them we can infer what the social organization of homo sapiens might have been like at the dawn of evolution of the human difference. Anthropologists (Eliade, 1964; Nicholson, 1987) describe the remarkable similarity among tribal-spiritual based cultures with regard to how they view person and cosmos. The similarity seems to be that they are based on primordial mentation and its language, not on reflective representational thought, a fact that accounts for their similarity despite their isolation from one another, not only existentially in terms of geography and communication, but over the millennia as well. This is strong if inferential evidence that their social organization is based on a common mental structure and the language that reflects it.

The mental structure and language of one of these tribes, the Pirahã of the Amazon basin, has been described by Daniel Everett (2008), a missionary turned cultural anthropologist and linguist, and was recounted in several previous books (Robbins, 2011, 2018, in press). The Pirahã are hunter-gatherers. The tribal population is stable, consisting of perhaps 350 inhabitants living in a series of small villages on the Maici River, a tributary of the Amazon. Though small in number, the culture and language are remarkably resistant to outside influence, which has primarily intruded in the forms of Portuguese westernization and Christian missionary endeavors such as Everett's original initiative. Everett lived among them intermittently for several decades, first as a missionary and then, as his orientation changed from religious colonization to scientific curiosity and study, he became an anthropologically oriented linguist. He and his former wife, who divorced as their orientation toward being there diverged, may be the only outsiders to have mastered their difficult language, which has a prosodic bird-like singing and whistling quality with extraordinary subtle nuances. His descriptions are remarkable illustrations of a social collective based on primordial mental activity and its linguistic reflection.

The Pirahã share beliefs that to Western minds would be labeled hallucinatory and delusional. The beliefs of these peoples about themselves

58 Origins of social structure from mental structure

and the world appear to have limited relationship to their functional perceptual-cognitive abilities to navigate and survive in the natural environment they inhabit, abilities which actually surpass most members of contemporary cultures suddenly confronted with the need to survive in similar environments. Everett begins his 2008 book by recounting a remarkable example about being awakened one morning by the noise of the tribe, whose members were assembled on the banks of the Maici River. They were talking and gesturing excitedly about their god, who was apparently on the opposite bank. While such cultures, "lacking" in the capacity for reflective creative thought and some of its products such as science and technology, do not expand limitlessly as do contemporary Western cultures that tend to colonize others, they tend to maintain a state of homeostasis and equilibrium with the environment and its available resources. The functional difference between self-centric Western and socio-centric tribal cultures is not between reality and mythology, function and disfunction, but between relative preferences for reflective logical thought and for primordial mental activity, and their respective consequences.

These socio-centric or collective cultures do not differentiate a psychological self, separate from the cosmos. As a result, what we would call the natural world is animated and understood as quasi-human. In language and communication, they do not distinguish themselves from one another, the ancestral world from the immediate day-to-day world, or the living from the dead whose souls (not memories) live on within them. Ancestors are every bit as alive as existing members of one's family. Dreaming is just as concretely real as any other "reality" and is conceived as a particular kind of journey, involving time or space travel of the soul or spirit to another place or supernatural dimension, or even to a self that has been changed, for example, into another person or animal. Such experiences are looked upon as ominous or portentous encounters that provide information about being in the world. The soul or spirit is not believed to be a psychic quality but rather an essence that can travel in time and space. What Westerners call death or termination of individual life is in spiritual cultures the permanent severance of the relationship between the soul and body. Similar though attenuated aspects of such beliefs can be found in the belief systems of some religions in Western society. Memory is lacking; life is rooted in the immediate present, without a sense of past or future.

According to Everett, "Pirahã culture constrains communication to non-abstract subjects which fall within the immediate experience of interlocutors" (2005, p. 621). He calls this the *immediacy of experience principle* (2008), and I would say it is a reflection of concreteness and enactment rather than reflective thought and symbolization. The Pirahã live entirely in the present moment in which reality is synonymous with immediate sensory-perceptual-motor experience. They make frequent use of a particular adjective/adverb to express

Origins of social structure from mental structure **59**

something entering or leaving immediate perception, and if something or someone is out of sight it or they are absent from discourse until again concretely present. Pirahã language expresses what is and not what was or will be or what might be; there is no concept of time, past or future. It is what it is and is not used symbolically to represent other things. In other words, the mental structure and language are characterized by fleeting imagery and lack stable representations.

Pirahã have no trouble navigating through life; places are identified not by a symbolic mental map but by their concrete presence to things like the personal activity that is or was done there, or by a concrete identifying geographical feature or a kind of vegetation or wildlife found there.

In this world of concrete immediacy there is no conception of time past, present, and imagined future, and no apparent sense of logical sequence, causality, or consequences. It follows that there is no memory in the sense of something that happened at another time, and no collective history. This is not equivalent to saying there is no sense of things past, for there are accounts of what has actually been experienced by someone, but it is talked about as though it is a happening in the present moment. There is no anticipation or planning. For example, they do not stockpile goods for a future time when they might be needed.

This literal quality, lacking symbolism or analogy, was illustrated when a native asked Everett why a visitor was applying insect repellent and he responded with a kind of charade by imitating the flight, sound, and sting of the insects, and concluded by slapping an imaginary mosquito, only to see the native observers turn to Everett in puzzlement and ask why the man was hitting himself.

It is not surprising, then, that the Pirahã have no written language, which requires a degree of mental representation and symbolic capacity to construct, even if the words themselves can subsequently be used concretely, at times, as things, as are expletives. And their spoken language lacks abstract qualitative descriptors. For example, while the natives are sensitive and responsive to color cues, they do not have abstract words for colors. Instead, they substitute likeness or identity. The object is not "red," it is called blood. They do not remember the name of a visitor; instead, he or she is dubbed by the name of a Pirahã whose features bear some resemblance. Their language has few pronouns; instead, they refer to concrete and specific names.

Pirahã language also lacks numbers and sequential counting or quantifying concepts, another instance of absence of logic and abstraction. Even after Everett and his family conducted months of classes with the natives none were able to count to ten or add 1+1. This was not for lack of motivation, for it had been demonstrated to them that such learning might have value in helping them to negotiate more effectively with Portuguese traders with whom they have considerable commerce.

60 Origins of social structure from mental structure

What westerners might think about as ideas, to the Pirahã are things, placed adjacent to one another, sequenced by contiguity or affect state rather than by temporal or causal logic. There are no subordinate clauses in Pirahã speech, no recursive combining of one idea within another in a sentence.

Pirahã language contains few kinship terms, and kinship bonds such as marriage are loosely maintained and very much of the moment. This does not mean they do not care about one another. The most likely explanation is that they do not have a sense of temporal continuity or enduring representations of the relevant ideational commitments and their emotional basis. Someone who is gone from immediate sight or hearing is no longer a subject of internal connection, although he or she is readily recognized on return. While the Pirahã show affect and are generally a playful people who help one another out in practical matters, they do not seem to be aware of enduring emotions about one another in the sense of enduring representations or emotional states that are necessary for more abstract notions of attachment. Where emotions of anger might be expected there is instead action or enactment, usually in the form of distance or disengagement, and preoccupation with other aspects of immediate experience than the relationship.

Out of sight is out of mind. Everett's visits to the Pirahã have been by float plane, landing on the Maici River. The Pirahã are excited by this phenomenon each time it occurs and respond by making airplane models out of balsa wood. Each event is immediate, stimulus bound, and short-lived. It soon ceases and the natives lose interest in the models and the model making; apparently there is no abstract or memorial significance, and nothing remains to be thought about.

Everett recounts vivid experiences about how Pirahã deal with death and child rearing that are also consistent with a hypothesis of primordial language including absence of emotional representation, of a sense of time past and future, and of consequences. A woman died a protracted death in breech childbirth while observers seemed unaware of the consequences of what was happening and apparently viewed her pain discontinuously as a thing of the moment and experienced no guilt or concern about her future fate. Everett recorded subsequent dialogue with her husband who repeated over and over words like "she is not here now" accompanied by tone and behavior that conveyed his obvious distress but was devoid of awareness of the permanence of the loss or the need to grieve that would follow from awareness based on a stable mental-emotional representation of a separate person.

Infants and small children are given what to Western eyes is an unusual degree of freedom to do whatever they want. A Westerner might interpret this as enlightened non-helicopter parenting, but it is reflective of "out of sight is out of mind," and lack of predictive awareness of possible future consequences. Everett notes the absence of punishment for forbidden behavior and of protection from harm, both of which involve a sense of time and ability

Origins of social structure from mental structure **61**

to think logically about consequences. He observed a scene where an infant played with a sharp knife, risking self-mutilation, in the presence of seemingly unconcerned adults. Infants are nursed until the arrival of another child, often around four years, and then weaned abruptly and entirely, often screaming for nights on end while parents, nursing the new baby, seem oblivious. Ordinary Western conclusions about such behaviors, for example, that the Pirahã don't care about one another, are belied by their close community and affectionate and helping attitudes toward one another. Everett's interpretation is that they have a high degree of respect for one another's individuality and autonomy. He points to the degree of self-sufficiency adults manifest. This seems to me an implausible hypothesis as they seem unaware of others' separateness and its consequences. It seems more likely that they lack an abstract conception of causality and consequence and are concrete and stimulus bound.

Pirahã is a spiritual culture, but not in the sense of reflective thought that characterizes Western stories and myths. There is no fantasy and no shared cultural fiction or mythology. Pirahã mental activity seems devoid of the qualities of abstraction and symbolization that westerners assume when defining something as a myth. They do not make art or tell stories that involve imagination or fantasy. They do tell stories of a kind, but these involve recounting experiences within the sensory-perceptual lifetime of the person, told as though they are happening currently. And yet Pirahã believe themselves to be shape-changers, undifferentiated from spirits in the cosmos. There is an active spirit or dream world that they "see," believe, and participate in waking and sleeping, that to them is quite real. Their attitude toward dreams is that they are another kind of immediate real experience or journey. Behavior that to the Western observer seems to involve supernatural mythological beliefs and practices requiring symbolic capacity is concrete to the Pirahã. The spirit world is experienced in dreaming and is contacted through transit into dreaming and though death; the tribe was able to "see" the spirit they called Xigagai.

The Pirahã sleeping pattern might be related to the absence of boundary between primordial mental activity in dreaming and in waking life. They have no clear demarcation between a time to sleep and a time to be awake, and generally sleep for an hour or two at a time throughout a 24-hour period. This might suggest an absence of psychological boundaries between the two states.

The Pirahã have been unable or unwilling to learn other languages even though they have been exposed to outsiders for several centuries, especially Portuguese. They refer to themselves concretely as "straight heads," in contrast to those who speak other languages who are "crooked heads." Their behavior and mentation cannot be a matter of genetic inbreeding of neurological defect, for although the Pirahã do not allow marriage outside the tribe it is accepted that their women are sexually active with outsiders, particularly

62 Origins of social structure from mental structure

the Portuguese traders. Hence, their gene pool is always expanding and not entirely inbred.

Human social structure gradually evolved from socio-centric to self-centric as human mental structure gradually evolved in complexity to include a second mental structure, reflective representational thought, in addition to the primordial structure we share with our primate ancestors. The next chapter uses what records humans have left behind of our species history to describe the course of this social evolution.

10

HISTORY OF THE PARALLEL EVOLUTION OF THE SECOND MENTAL STRUCTURE AND THE MOVEMENT OF HUMAN SOCIAL ORGANIZATION FROM SOCIO-CENTRIC TO SELF-CENTRIC

The second mental structure that constitutes the human difference, and its language, seem to have originated in parallel from a combination of biological evolution and the two things it produced, a larger more complex brain and vocal apparatus, and neoteny, that enabled and required learning through interaction with caregivers of a second mental process that in turn enabled the acquisition, accumulation, and intergenerational transmission of knowledge.

Human social structure has gradually evolved from organization based on persons sharing the primordial structure in order to equilibrate and maintain the social organization, to one based predominantly on the second mental structure, reflective representational thought, that is centered around the welfare, wants and needs of the individual. Acquisition of the ability to write has enabled humankind to leave for posterity an historical record of this evolution.

In the pre-linguistic era, humans probably made use of sounds that became antecedents of words, at the same time they inscribed the images that comprise cave art. These lack a cohesive sequential grammatical structure. They are products of the first mental structure, and their communicative meaning is biologically programmed. However, from the beginning of speciation, homo sapiens possessed speech centers that enabled transmission of increasingly nuanced meanings from one member to another that eventually evolved into words and sentences. In the course of evolution of civilization, humans moved from a kind of communication that must have been based on spoken instrumental signals related to concrete events of the moment to simple signing. From the use of signs, the capacity to reflect, symbolize, record, track the passage of time, and communicate with others must have evolved. This enabled communication when parties were no longer in visual proximity but

DOI: 10.4324/9781003435785-10

64 Parallel evolution of the second mental structure

at a distance. It was part of a complexity that gradually included things like reflection and symbolization, phonetic linkages that unite speaking and writing, and the cursive writing that made the written word almost as easy to use for communication as the spoken. Invention of alphabets, consisting of characters that have symbolic and phonetic linkage, was one of the major later developments and made it possible for humans to construct sentences and written language. In the process, what hitherto were oral narrative traditions related to the concrete undifferentiated beliefs about person and cosmos became the stories. Then it became possible to represent and reflect on what was hitherto belief or mythology, to recognize the difference between stories and real happenings, and to deliberately create fiction.

How did these civilizations, and the minds that created them, evolve from stable mostly biologically determined social organizations based on the primordial mental structure of earliest homo sapiens? Cave art, the first enduring manifestation of uniquely human intelligence, was most likely the result of literal efforts to reproduce mental images. The oldest discovered cave art, the most ancient known homo sapiens document, dates back not quite 50,000 years, meaning that the remarkable difference between humans and other species has evolved in a comparatively brief span of time in relation to the history of earth and even the history of living species. The usual subject of this art is large animals, seemingly reflective of mental images related to the chase – the hunter-gatherer culture of the artists. It resembles the transient carvings of float planes described in an earlier chapter that Pirahã natives made after each arrival of outsiders. A spelunker on a remote Indonesian island discovered a notable exception when he lived out what might have been a scene from an Indiana Jones movie. He spied a hole in the ceiling of a cave and clambered up to it only to discover a large hall containing what is at this writing the world's oldest example of cave art, dating back at least 43,900 years, about 20,000 years prior to the famous depictions of animals and humans in caves in Lascaux, France. In contrast to the realism of the French paintings, those in the Indonesian cave depict eight figures that are part human and part animal or monster, hunting wild pigs and dwarf buffaloes (anoas). Perhaps this reflects the beginnings of recorded mythology in the form of animistic conceptions of the world.

Nearly 40,000 years elapsed after the creation of these images before the date of the first traces that have been discovered of civilization. Evidence of Sumerian culture has been found dating to 5500–4500 BC in Mesopotamia, at the junction of the Tigris and Euphrates rivers. This is the area now known as Iraq. Evidence of civilization dating to approximately the same time has been found in the Indus River Valley in what is now Pakistan and Afghanistan, and the upper and lower Nile that became ancient Egypt.

Perhaps a millennium later, still prior to the advent of the Christian calendar, civilizations arose in the Andes (3200 AD), and in the area around the Aegean Sea (Cycladic, 3300 AD) including the Minoan (2700 AD) and Mycenaean (1600 AD). Signs of civilization have been found in North Africa (Kerma, 2500 AD; and Kush 1070 AD), around the Yellow River Valley in China (Xia, 2070 AD; Shang, 1600 AD); and then the Zhou and Han dynasties. The breathtaking conclusion from this data is that human culture and civilization emerged more or less simultaneously in many parts of the world, suggesting it was driven by the forces of biological evolution; in this instance, the knowledge accumulating as a result of neoteny and the dependent learning relationship between children and caregivers. The pace of civilized change in the relatively brief subsequent period of recorded history and communication is equally astonishing by contrast, as though one abandoned the horse and buggy and put the pedal to the floor of a modern sports car.

The advent of civilization evolved along with the human acquisition of a second mental process, reflective thought, and involved a critical shift in human social organization that set it apart from the social organization of other species, and that of tribal human beings at the dawn of evolution from our primate ancestors. Hitherto, humans, like other animals, congregated in small local groups – herds, flocks, packs, bands, hives, colonies – there are many names for such groups depending on the species. Civilization enabled a qualitative advance in communication from that involving immediate local contact to contact at a distance, and social organization expanded to include complex interaction and evolution among and between groups.

Biological forces alone cannot have wrought such changes. Biological differences – in the brain, the speech apparatus, and maturation (neoteny) – are fundamental, but the subsequent developments are the consequences of the uniquely human capacity for learning and the acquisition and intergenerational transmission of knowledge that the lengthy period of extra-uterine maturation has enabled and required.

The Shabaka stone, dating to the first Egyptian dynasty around 3100 BC, is perhaps the oldest relic of the beginning transition to reflective thought. A major source of data for the period from 2600 to 2100 BC is the Pyramid texts, which were discovered on walls and sarcophagi. The Maxims of Ptahhotep, dating from around 2300 BC; the Coffin texts written on coffins from around 2100 BC; the Sinai inscriptions, dating from 1800 to 1500 BC; and the Amarna letters, 382 cuneiform clay tablets that served as communications between rulers in Egypt and Anatolia, are other early well-known historical sources. In Sumerian culture in Mesopotamia, as well as in Egypt, the Sinai, Canaan and South Arabia, China, Anatolia, Ethiopia, and Mesoamerica, alphabet-like writing systems developed somewhere between the third and second millennia BC. The elements that comprise written language differ from one culture to another. For example, hieroglyphic, hieratic and demotic are concepts that refer to the inscriptions of ancient Egypt and combine pictographs (representational pictures), and ideographs.

66 Parallel evolution of the second mental structure

Ideographs and logographs, or logograms, are character symbols without an associated phonetic quality. They represent words, as in Chinese or Japanese characters, or numerals. The first pure alphabets enabling linking single characters, creation of symbolic meaning, and single phonemes, emerged the first several hundred years of the second millennium BC in Egypt. The first evidence of hieratic, demotic cursive writing appears during that time, suggesting the integration and continuity characteristic of language, written or spoken.

Wim Van Den Dungen (2019), a Dutch epistemologist and anthropologist whose intellectual roots include Freud, Piaget, and Julian Jaynes, studied the evolution of Egyptian language from hieroglyphic signs to more complex language. His analysis led him to infer their initial language conformed to that of the primordial mental structure – concrete, undifferentiated, unintegrated and immediate, enactive and operational, and animistic. It is the language of recounted adventures that are not yet recognized to be myths or stories. The *Epic of Gilgamesh,* from around 2100 BC, is generally cited as the first evidence of cursive writing and of records that do not differentiate the inner world of the narrator from external reality. It is a story presumably written about a real ruler who undertakes a heroic journey, in the course of which he encounters gods and monsters.

Western civilization commenced as part of a gradual movement north from the cradle of civilization in the Middle East over the course of approximately 1500 years. Around 800–700 BC evidence of a Greek alphabet can be found. The Roman alphabet and Indo-European so-called Romance languages evolved around year zero of the Christian calendar.

The major source of Greek literature is the epic poetry of Homer that we think of, from the perspective of reflective thought, as mythic but audiences probably heard as actual adventures. Homer codified orally transmitted stories of adventures that had been conceived of by a primordial mental process prior to the advent of reflective thought and the separation of story from reality that it enabled. In his introduction to the 1990 Fagles translation of the *Iliad,* Bernard Knox, one of the foremost scholars of Greek mythology and drama, informs us that these were conceived of prior to the advent of written language. Bennet Simon (1978) and Bruno Snell (1982) have speculated about the minds of these pre-literate peoples from analysis of the records left us by Homer and Sophocles. The fact that the characters had names and histories and engaged in actions is misleading to contemporary Western readers because the concept of individual person separate from the cosmos, possessor of a reflective mind, did not exist. In these adventures there is no first-person pronoun "I," and there are no terms for body, mind, self or gender and no personal pronouns. Entities considered separate and distinct in reflective representational thought; including mind (psyche), body, specific emotions, contemplated thoughts, and actions; are not clearly distinguished from

Parallel evolution of the second mental structure **67**

actions and attitudes. In lieu of a language for emotions, their precursors are expressed somatically by affectively tinged facial expressions, gestures, and actions. Motivational forces are conceived of as external events and causes. Punishment of the hero's misdeeds by the gods is an enactment of what in reflective thought might be a sense of guilt. The gods and their actions, might each be articulate in reflective thought as particular emotions (wrath, greed, envy, lust, retribution, and punishment), depicted as conflicts among gods or heroes rather than as internal conflicts (I want to do this, but I should do that). Mortal heroes are distinguished by the particular gods and goddesses who favor or undermine them; in modern terms, undifferentiated projections. Odysseus literally navigates between Scylla (lust, wish-fulfillment) and Charybdis (destructive impulses), opposed by Poseidon but aided by Athena in his effort to keep on the straight and narrow pathway home. No wonder the contemporary Western reader is left with the impression that the loves and hates of Greek deities seems very much like the sometimes-petty squabbles of human beings. Language is concrete, as evinced by the magical power of curses, proclaimed by the gods, to transform reality.

The Oedipus tale is about a crossroads of life, but it is unlike, for example, Robert Frost's poems *The Road Not Taken* and *Stopping by Woods on a Snowy Evening* (Lathem, 1969), where Frost is clearly reflecting about critical life choices. Frost's poems represent the choice about career in *Road Not Taken*, and between life and death in *Stopping by Woods*. The author assumes the reader will interpret the poetry symbolically, as allegory or metaphor. Sophocles' Oedipus, in contrast, makes literal choices in his adventure, discovering the consequences in action; unable to reflect in advance about a future and its possibilities. Metaphoric interpretation waited about 2,500 years until the advent of the second mental process and Freud's re-telling of the story as one of child development in which fantasies of fratricide and incest are resolved by awareness of the law of the father, thoughtful choice, repression and control.

In reflective thought such epics are looked upon as mythology because we choose to read them as conscious products of imagination. However, the Greeks of the time when these narratives were conceived were recounting what they believed to be actual adventures in the undifferentiated animated way they comprehended the cosmos. A current-day iteration of this distinction that makes it easier to understand can be found in Christian theological debates about whether Biblical stories are literal histories of God, Jesus, death and resurrection, and so forth, or are parables or metaphors meant to have symbolic emotional significance.

Although self-centric culture based on the second mental process did not have a major impact on Western mind and behavior until around the time of the industrial revolution, it makes its first recorded appearance in Athens of the fifth and sixth centuries BC. Anticipating Kant and Freud two and a half

68 Parallel evolution of the second mental structure

millennia later, Sophocles separated psyche (mind or soul) from body (soma), divided soul into three structures; logistikon (thought or reason), thumoedes, spirit or passion (affects), and the basest animal or appetitive part, epithumeikon; and located them in different parts of the body. The cognitive part was believed to be situated in the head, the passionate part in the chest, and the appetitive part in the gut. The passionate part is described as sensory-perceptual, sensual, concrete, unbounded, and responsible for dreaming, very much like Freud's primary process and primordial mental structure. It was believed to be the mental operation of childhood as well.

In India at approximately the same time, 600 BC, Siddhartha, the Buddha, was also conceptualizing a primordial mental process with sociocentric ramifications in which selfhood or self-satisfaction is an illusion to be dissolved in the quest for selflessness or undifferentiation of person from universe.

In approximately the same period BC, in the area around Sumerian Babylon, ancient myths about journeys, Gods, death, and rebirth similar to and perhaps derived from the *Epic of Gilgamesh* were being re-written in the form of what later became the Old Testament of the Christian Bible.

Greek influence on language and mythology slowly wended its way north with the Etruscans, to the Roman Empire and Latin language, and then to the Romance languages of modern Europe.

The Roman Empire collapsed around AD 500 and was followed by the era of modern religion. The Biblical New Testament was written in Egypt, and perhaps soon thereafter, influenced by it, the Muslim Quran. The millennium known as the Dark Ages followed: it was a world understood according to the primordial mental structure that didn't conceive of persons as separate from the social system or distinguish reality from belief. Any sign of individuality, independence, or reflective empirical reasoning was defined as evil and dangerous, a kind of mental illness then thought of as heresy and the work of the Devil, as it threatened the church's sociocentric control over its followers. Mind was not to be differentiated from the mythological beliefs defined as the will of God. What we now call evolution was God's creation of man. In AD 397, Saint Augustine articulated a view of human mind and inner life that included the struggle between selfless socio-centric conformity defined as goodness, and what we would now call individual freedom, but in the eyes of the church was evil bestiality or original sin. The goal of religion was selfless function of persons as cogs or parts in the social structure as the church defined it, with constant vigilance to root out the evil of demonic possession, individuality, *Malleus Maleficarum*.

In that era people, lived their entire lives in the small communities into which they were born, and within which they were looked upon parts, not as individuals. There was no need for surnames identifying them as separate individuals. After the Norman conquest in Britain in AD 1066, however, the population began to expand and the use of surnames for identification commenced, reflecting the birth of individuality. But the surnames had to do with categories and attachments to larger organizations of which the person was part, not to individual personality characteristics. They related to things like lineage in relation to the king, fiefdom, and in many instances, the work the person performed. The origin of many surnames (Barber, Carpenter, Tailor, Fisher, Hunter, Skinner, Cook, Mason, etc.) that persist today came from the occupations of these people that were then used to refer to them.

Around the twelfth and thirteenth centuries the intellectual awakening known as Scholasticism commenced in Western Europe. St. Thomas Aquinas resurrected the idea of an individual self and the tripartite idea of soul, mind, and body. However, there was no major social change in the relationship between person and social group until the Renaissance that began in the fifteenth century and the Reformation that began about a century later, around 1500, when the traditional rigid Procrustean bond in which persons were more or less interchangeable components in a social group began to loosen. Humans began to be looked upon as separate individuals with rights, freedoms, and goals distinct from those of more powerful group authority. The secular or self-centric mode of thinking based on a second mental structure, with science and rationality as its masthead, initiated the transition from holistic groups in which people are component parts to social organizations governed by the needs and wants of individual members. Social organizations competed for dominance, as did alternative ways of viewing the relationship between persons and the larger world by means of either the primordial mental structure or reflective thought. This began to supersede the unity based on the primordial mental structure alone.

The remarkable shift from the primordial mental structure to reflective thought that is at the core of separate individual selfhood produced what we think of as civilization, the large division thereof that we think of as science and technology on the one hand; philosophy and literature, on the other; and more recently, the social sciences that combine both. Manifestations of primordial mentation did not cease, however. They continued to make themselves manifest in such things as religion, and many other social groupings based on belief rather than reflection, "fact" and logic.

In order to understand the shift in predominant mental process it is instructive to compare two giants of the Renaissance, Leonardo da Vinci, and Nicolaus Copernicus, who lived around the same time, mid-1400s to mid-1500s. Copernicus constructed perhaps the first theory built around reflection and the conception of a universe "out there" functioning according to principles different than the subjective beliefs of its beholders. While his discoveries related to astronomy, his more fundamental innovation was conceptualizing relativity. His model of a universe de-centered from human

70 Parallel evolution of the second mental structure

anthropomorphizing replaced the accepted Ptolemaic cosmology in which the actions of the heavenly bodies were not differentiated from immediate human sensory experience and beliefs based upon it. He conceived of a reality separate and independent from the subjectivity of the observer.

However, Leonardo da Vinci, who lived in the latter half of the fourteenth century and early into the 1500s, seems to have been between the two mental processes. Da Vinci is at once considered a great artist and one of the first scientists and technicians. Perhaps, if it makes any sense to make such comparisons, he was greater than Copernicus; some would say the greatest genius ever. Da Vinci was a sensitive detailed observer of the world around him who depicted in meticulous artistic detail the earth, the heavenly bodies, the human body, and machines. From his imagination he designed remarkable machines, many of which appear to be forerunners of more modern inventions. However, he had a limited conception of a reality consisting of external forces and interactions that existed independent of his beliefs, so he did not understand the need to do experimental testing and verification of his ideas. As a result, most of his creations such as the screw-propelled flying craft were totally impractical. However, recent discoveries suggest he had an experimental understanding of gravity and had begun to devise mathematical equations about it that presage Newton.

Relativity and the need to create a model that differentiated the internal operations of the self from the forces, actions, and consequences of an external world, gradually replaced Ptolemy's model of the universe which centered around the earth. Scientists began to study, model, and reflect upon an external world differentiated from the self. Only half a century after da Vinci, the work of Galileo Galilei, who lived between the mid-1500s and mid-1600s, was based on meticulous experimental testing and verification rather than undifferentiated belief. It was securely ensconced in principles of relativity and concepts of external forces of gravity, speed and velocity, movement and balance, measurement of terrestrial and celestial direction and motion, and the like. Galileo was convicted in the Inquisition for teachings heretical to those of the Bible, especially related to the concept of a solar system centered around natural forces rather than around God.

By the time of Isaac Newton and his discovery of the laws of motion and gravity, from the mid-seventeenth to the mid-eighteenth centuries, the discipline of science, based on reflective thought, had been thoroughly defined and mostly separated from the hitherto-prevalent conception of an undifferentiated anthropomorphic universe whose causality was attributed to a deity (Aristotle's prime mover) and defined by rigid religious doctrine. However, as recently as 1857, Darwin's hypothesis of evolution of species based on meticulous observation came under attack from the creationists who continued to maintain that God made man in his image. A substantial number of people continue to harbor that belief.

Science spawned technology. And it was technology that produced the industrial revolution that began in the mid-1700s and was responsible for population shifts including immigration and the movement to cities. These developments permanently loosened the socio-centric stranglehold of the church and marked the advent of self-centric Western culture largely created by the second mental structure.

The leap in civilization enabled by reflective thought and individual-centeredness was marked not only by the advent of science and technology, but by sea changes in literature and philosophy. The social world of primordial mentation included telling stories which were very real to the participants but that we now look upon as myths. The world that was depicted, for example in the Homeric epics, was not differentiated from the thoughts and feelings we now look upon as originating within the self. As humans developed a second mental structure individual expression and social communication began to shift to story-telling that involved imagination and was based on symbolization. The world of visual art and of fiction writing that began around the period known as the Enlightenment was highlighted by Shakespeare's psychological dramas, written around 1600, that vividly exemplify the growing preoccupation with the individual person and his or her "internal" psychology.

In 1619 René Descartes, then a young man, was distressed by three vivid dreams he had one night and puzzled about how he might differentiate reality from fantasy, waking from sleeping. This incident was the inception of his philosophy. In 1637 he published the *Discourse on Method,* in which he proposed his revolutionary understanding of reflective thinking, based on self-doubt and questioning of the veracity of purely sensory experience such as is characteristic of dreaming, or primordial mental activity. His emphasis on the central role of reflective thought is characterized by the phrase "Dubito, ergo cognito, ergo sum"; I doubt, therefore I think, therefore I am. Descartes' view of human complexity – persons considered both as subject and object of reflection, and persons separate from others who are also separate beings with their own centers – represents one of those iconic paradigm shifts. He challenged the undifferentiated god-centric or solar-centric universe of primordial mental activity in a way that changed the direction of culture and society.

The leap in civilization enabled by reflective thought and individual centeredness was marked by a transformation in literature and philosophy. Shakespeare's psychological dramas demonstrate the growing preoccupation with the individual person and his or her "internal" psychology. Cassius might have been an historian of the shift from animism to intrapsychic reflection when he remarked "the fault, dear Brutus, lies not in our stars but in ourselves."

In his 1725 treatise *Scienza Nuova,* Giambattista Vico introduced a spiral metaphor to illustrate his concepts of repetition and progress, both central to the notions of time, memory, and linear change that are fundaments of reflective thought.

Whereas the scientific revolution launched during the Enlightenment explored the nature of the world around us, Immanuel Kant (1787) studied the nature of mind in society. He postulated that mind is a tripartite structure comprising reason, understanding, and sensibility or judgment (1787). He described what we know and cannot know, and examined how we as individuals within society are obligated to act physically, logically, and morally. In his *Anthropology From a Pragmatic Point* of View, written in 1798, Kant examined the nature of consciousness and self-consciousness. In a 1784 treatise entitled *An Answer to the Question: What is Enlightenment?,* written in response to the susceptibility of the masses to novel scientific theories, he argues that because humans possess the faculty of reflective thought, we have the duty to think critically. He concluded that if every rational being used his capacity for reflective thought, the result would be a true "…age of enlightenment.'" His work was both the forerunner of modern cognitive science, and laid the groundwork for Freud's creation of the discipline of psychoanalysis, based on reflection and awareness of the similarity between one's mind and that of others.

11
THE STRUCTURAL DIFFERENCE BETWEEN NEUROSIS AND PSYCHOSIS

The theory and practice of psychoanalysis that Freud created is an outgrowth of social organization based on the second mental structure and a culture of self-reflection. Another unique feature of the lengthy period of immaturity and dependence on caregivers unique to humans is the manifestation psychoanalysis was created to study and ameliorate, individual human destructiveness.

Freud understood the underpinning of psychopathology to be the result of conscious or repressed conflict among what he believed to be the three psychic structures: id, ego, and superego. His understanding was limited by the fact that the discipline of sociology was in its infancy at the time he formulated his theories, and he was unaware of the fact that there were other social organizations beyond the authoritarian European culture in which he lived. This contextual limitation, and the fact that his own personality was forged out of the crucible of this culture, left him unaware of the limitations of his developmental preoccupation with paternal authority and the fundamental importance of mothers and the developmental phases of attachment and separation. In particular, he focused on the Oedipal conflict around three years of age. He believed that failure to resolve the Oedipal complex led to the major human psychopathology, psychoneurosis, based on repression of the conflict to an unconscious realm or state and disguised re-emergence of the problem in the form of symptoms, inhibitions and anxiety. Such a view fails to account for psychosis (Robbins, 2019), and has limited the scope of psychoanalysis to neurosis; pathology based on the capacity to experience and repress intrapsychic conflict. While he understood in principle that events in earlier infancy were also important determinants of adult personality, they remained in a somewhat mysterious terra incognita, a realm called "pre-Oedipal." For reasons about which we can only speculate, Freud failed to understand the

DOI: 10.4324/9781003435785-11

central importance of mothers in development, hence the role of attachment to and separation from in the maturational process. Thus psychosis, pathology based on the primordial mental structure that is undifferentiated and unintegrated, has remained for the most part beyond the scope of psychoanalysis.

Over the century or more of its evolution various psychoanalysts including Otto Rank, Sandor Ferenczi, Melanie Klein, Donald Winnicott, Ronald Fairbairn, John Bowlby, and Margaret Mahler attempted to revise and expand psychoanalytic theory to account for the importance of earlier development, and some of them for psychosis. Freud had proposed a model of the primary process in 1900 and even asserted that it is the mentation of infancy and psychosis, but he did not elaborate its applicability to psychosis and in his various writings still thought about it as a genetic inability to make a relationship (transference) and to construct and maintain ego function (Robbins, 2019). His view has been challenged in part, but fundamentally psychoanalysis remains a theory of neurosis that assumes the ability to distinguish self from other (form a transference) and sufficient cohesion and integration to experience and resolve intrapsychic conflict.

A normal/neurotic person has developed the awareness of self and other as separate individuals, including the ability to distinguish his or her inner life from that of others, and is able to experience and resolve emotional conflicts among contradictory emotionally saturated ideas either in a conscious way or by using a combination of repression, inhibition, and symptomatic expression. He or she is able to live independently, which involves negotiating a world where persons are differentiated from one another, and the self is sufficiently organized to be regulated and managed as a cohesive entity. Although in the instance of neurosis the internal resolution may limit satisfaction and success. Psychosis, in contrast, is a condition arising from pathology of attachment, leading to inability to achieve self-other differentiation from the primary caregiver, and inability to integrate a separate self that is capable of thoughtful representation of experience and reflective self-awareness. The result is varying extremes of difficulty living independently, working, and establishing stable relationships in the world. In other words, the understanding and functioning of psychotic persons remains mostly based on the primordial mental structure even though living in the adult world requires both the ability to function predominantly according to the second mental structure, and the flexibility to move back and forth between one structure and another as circumstantial adaptation requires.

As a consequence of inability to recognize and resolve conflict internally, the psychotic person lives in a place where an undifferentiated world/self becomes the stage for destructive enactments. Not surprisingly, psychosis usually comes to social attention at one of three nodal points in the life cycle in which maturation requires a step toward separation and individuation, because such transitions require an integrated cohesive sense of self and a realistic capacity to distinguish others as separate persons. The first such nodal point occurs at the time children are expected to separate from home to begin school. The second is when adolescents or young adults leave home in a more permanent way to begin advanced education or work. Finally, there are adults who have formally left home and live on their own and function more or less independently but are unable to take the further step of forming and sustaining a close relationship and beginning families of their own and creating a stable productive work life.

Failure of the first separation produces child psychosis; failure of the second separation produces the signs and symptoms of schizophrenia and other severe mental ills. Failure at the third stage of separation reveals a psychotic personality organization that has been mostly concealed from the social world of the sufferer with a false self-organization. This social façade may be extremely effective, and from an external vantage point the person may seem unusually gifted and accomplished. This condition usually goes under such names as borderline, schizoid, sociopathic, or narcissistic personality; severe drug addiction; or unexpected suicide. I lump these conditions under the rubric of psychotic personality disorder because in intimate personal settings such as a close relationship, or a psychoanalytic treatment situation, the person functions in the mentation of primordial consciousness.

The following three case examples illustrate the difference between maladaptive functioning according to the primordial mental structure that underlies psychosis and more adaptive functioning according to the structure of reflective representational thought that underlies neurosis. The first, ironically, consists of one of the case reports published by Freud himself that he believed illustrates neurosis, but in fact illustrates psychosis. The next two are persons I treated in prolonged intensive psychoanalytic therapy. The first of these, Caroline, made steps to move from primordial mentation to reflective representational thought but these were limited and she was unable to sustain them. The second case of Sara describes a successful transition from the maladaptive primordial structure that was killing her to a thoughtful structure that allowed her to live a very successful, meaningful life.

Freud's case of the Rat Man

Freud's 1909 report of a patient he called the "Rat Man" describes his treatment a young man named Ernest Lanzer. The title was derived from Lanzer's sadistic frightening obsessive belief that a rat was gnawing the anuses of his lady friend Constanza and his father, who had in fact died nine years previously. The belief was so real and compelling that Lanzer had to concoct equally obsessive counter measures magically designed to keep it from happening.

The symptoms that brought Lanzer to Freud appeared in his twenties as a consequence of paralyzing obsessional ambivalence about whether to marry

76 The structural difference between neurosis and psychosis

Constanza, the woman he believed he loved, or to marry a wealthy, socially well-connected woman who had somehow been chosen for him. His father, who had died nine years earlier and from whom Lanzer had hoped to get a large inheritance, had once faced a similar dilemma and resolved it by marrying for money.

The case is unique insofar as it is the only one in which Freud left notes of sessions that enable us to get a retrospective sense of the data from which his formulations came. In his report Freud unwittingly gives an excellent portrayal of the difference between the mental structure underlying psychosis and the structure responsible for neurosis. Freud was determined to prove and illustrate his theory, so he spelled it out in detail and tried to educate his skeptical patient, who dramatized the primordial structure, to accept it. Ironically, the clinical data Freud presents, and even various observations he made, support both a psychotic diagnosis and the much better fit of his model of primary process mentation that he noted underlies psychosis.

Freud's intention was to use the report to illustrate the hypothesis that unconscious repressed conflicts with authority, in this instance Lanzer's father, over infantile sexuality related to anal eroticism and masturbation, were responsible for his symptoms. Both in his interactions with Lanzer and his written report Freud selectively focused on aspects of the patient's childhood related to his anal and genital psychosexual development and his relationship with his father. While he recorded other interesting and probably pertinent aspects of Lanzer's history he did not figure them into his theorizing, so they do not have a sufficiently prominent detailed place to allow full understanding of their importance.

Freud's interpretation of Lanzer's obsessional belief that rats were gnawing the anuses of his father and Constanza, and another strange belief about payment for a pair of glasses he had ordered that he believed would counteract it, was that these were the symptoms of an unconscious repressed childhood conflict related to anal eroticism. He writes:

> The unconscious, I explained [to Lanzer], was the infantile; it was that part of the self which had become separated off from it in infancy, which had not shared the later stages of its development, and which had in consequence become repressed. It was the derivatives of this repressed unconscious that were responsible for the involuntary thoughts which constituted his illness.
>
> *(1909, pp. 163–164, bracketed comments mine)*

Lanzer was paralyzed by a sadomasochistic belief system that was concrete, involved body parts, and consisted of magical omnipotent ideas one of which was intended to counteract another. His obsessive thoughts were not differentiated from impulsive affect-driven motor actions and counter-actions

The structural difference between neurosis and psychosis **77**

or prohibitions related to doing and undoing that did not differentiate intrapsychic from external reality. He believed that these thoughts had the magical omnipotent power to alter reality. He was not able to hold two confusing or conflicting ideas in mind simultaneously. His ritualistic actions were intended to prevent his sadistic phantasies, ranging from anal torture to murder, from actually happening. They were mostly about his father, who was very much alive for him even though he had died nine years before, and the woman he was ambivalent about marrying. I use the term phantasy rather than fantasy as Klein did, to denote the quality of reality and belief rather than imagination.

Here are several examples from Lanzer's complaints: "He thought that a wish of his had actually kept his cousin alive on two occasions" (1909, p. 298). Lanzer lamented that if his cousin were actually ill then he would no longer have to worry about how his thoughts were keeping him healthy.

Another example of undifferentiated omnipotent belief was his neologism "glejsamen" which he used to keep the sadistic phantasies he had when masturbating from actually happening. The neologism condensed words from a prayer, the name of a place his father had visited, and the name of a woman friend. Freud comments: "the detailed account which the patient gave me of the external events of these days and of his reactions to them was full of self-contradictions and sounded hopelessly confused" (1909, p. 169). He had no conception of the passage of time or of the distinction between intrapsychic and external reality, for his dead father was very much alive and his beliefs and actions were either maintaining his life or killing him.

When Constanza left Lanzer during a time when he was studying for examinations, in order to be with her dying mother, he had a powerful obsessive urge to kill her mother and an equally compelling urge to slit his throat in order to undo it. He told Freud "If you received a command to take your examination this term at the first possible opportunity, you might manage to obey it. But if you were commanded to cut your throat with a razor, what then?" Freud adds that:

> He had at once become aware that this command had already been given and was hurrying to the cupboard to fetch his razor when he thought: 'No, it's not so simple as that. You must go and kill the old woman.' Upon that, he had fallen to the ground, beside himself with horror.
>
> *(p. 186)*

To fit his neurosis theory Freud recast the situation into the structure of reflective thought: the language of a fantasied wish, about which he had been conflicted, that he had repressed. He tried to convince Lanzer that what he had really thought, the flexibility to take himself as subject and as object: "'Oh, I should like to go and kill that old woman for robbing me of my love!'

78 The structural difference between neurosis and psychosis

Thereupon followed the command: 'Kill yourself, as a punishment for these savage and murderous passions!'" (p. 186).

Perhaps Lanzer's most bizarre psychotic delusion and hallucination, that Freud believed was a neurotic obsessive symptom, was a regular nocturnal interruption of his studies, when he would open the door to his apartment, believe that his dead father was watching, expose his genitalia and look at them in a mirror. Freud reasoned that Lanzer was expressing in this "symptom" repressed anger at his father.

Freud's selective attention to information related to Lanzer's psychosexual development and its possible relationship to his childhood beliefs about his father's authority kept him from paying much attention to the presence and possible role of anger and rage in Lanzer's development and pathology, and in a possible transference that impeded the treatment, although Freud recorded information about these things in his notes. They also diverted his attention from the possible role of his relationship to his mother in his pathology, which would be more consistent with the idea that difficulties in attachment and separation might have led to maladaptive persistence of a primordial mental structure.

There was a good deal of unacknowledged sadism and abuse in Lanzer's background, especially in stories his mother told him about her upbringing and in some punishments he received, especially from her. And Lanzer told Freud that he had seduced the young daughters of several of his friends, taking them on trips and entering their hotel bedrooms at night and masturbating them. He seemed to believe they had enjoyed it and to be unaware of his hostility toward women. Freud did not make much of this. During the course of his treatment Lanzer reported sadistic dreams and fantasies he had about Freud, albeit apparently with little affect. Lanzer seems to have been rather compliant during their sessions, if unconvinced of the validity of Freud's ideas, and Freud does not seem to have considered the question of hostile transference or of the possibility that Lanzer was coming from a position of primordial mentation in which he did not have mental representations of his emotions and reflective awareness of their presence. Freud writes "Strangely enough, his belief that he really nourished feelings of rage against his father has made no progress in spite of his seeing that there was every logical reason for supposing that he had those feelings" (1909, p. 306).

Freud's determination to prove his neurosis theory seems to have blinded him to the fact that his data clearly illustrated the model of primary process mentation that he had also noted (1900) is responsible for what he called the hallucinations and delusions characteristic of dreaming, and the mentation of psychosis. Yet he notes in his report that his patient's nocturnal dreams often seemed just like his waking obsessions. He writes:

> I refer to the omnipotence which he ascribed to his thoughts and feelings, and to his wishes, whether good or evil…. It is, I must admit, decidedly

The structural difference between neurosis and psychosis **79**

tempting to declare that this idea was a delusion and that it oversteps the limits of obsessional neurosis…this belief is a frank acknowledgement of a relic of the old megalomania of infancy.

(1909, pp. 232–233)

Caroline

The next example is excerpted from my 2002 paper on language and delusion in schizophrenia. Caroline was a diagnosed chronic schizoaffective schizophrenic, in and out of the major teaching hospital where she spent most of the decade following marginal completion of college. Most of the time she was severely regressed, catatonic, or else destructive and at times suicidal in response to delusions and auditory hallucinations.

Two courses of electro-convulsive therapy, numerous medications, and efforts at psychotherapy by a psychoanalyst were of no avail, and finally the treatment team concluded that they had nothing more to offer her and transferred her to the hospital where I began to work with her.

Caroline was eventually able to live more or less independently outside a hospital without the aid of medications, but she was never able to make a complete functional transition from primordial mentation to reflective representational thought. The ensuing discussion is intended to illustrate some of her transient attempts at transition.

Very shortly after her admission Caroline broke into the medication room on the ward and consumed a large quantity of drugs. She remained comatose and near death for several days. Many years later when she was no longer in the hospital and had begun to manifest some interest and capacity for reflective symbolic thought, she explained to me that she had been unable to tolerate the idea that she was like the other psychotic, dilapidated patients who inhabited the ward because they were "so out of it," so she decided to *get in* with the nurses and doctors. "So, I *broke in* to the med room. I was going to *get in*, maybe like the nurses, to their power."

In the hospital Caroline had the delusion she was the special patient and bride to be of the most important doctors, and that what would succeed in binding them to her was to be as regressed, passive and destructive as possible. Again, many years later, when she was able to reflect on her near suicide, she told me she had imagined her doctors had admired and been excited by the sight of her nude body comatose on the gurney. I gradually learned that the mantra she often repeated that "nothing good will ever happen" was not a despairing observation but a concrete statement of determination. Caroline created every kind of problem imaginable in her several years of hospitalization at the institution where I worked with her, and after discharge accidents, troubles with the law, destitution, and starvation. After years of treatment, we uncovered her unconscious envy of homeless

80 The structural difference between neurosis and psychosis

street-corner mendicants, for to her they epitomized success in tricking others to take care of them.

Much of the time I could not understand what she was talking about. One day, in a poorly concealed moment of despair and exasperation and without much thought, I remarked that she was speaking schizophrenese, a language I did not comprehend. She was taken aback, but not in the way one might expect. She casually informed me that as *I* was the therapist and *she* was the schizophrenic, it was *my* job to understand her. After unproductive discussions that spanned several sessions, I suddenly had the liberating thought that whether or not she chose to learn from me, I was not trapped in a hopeless situation. I could terminate with her or learn from her, and I told her that I would choose the latter course, and she would henceforth educate me about schizophrenese, and I would take notes, like a student.

In retrospect, this must have given her a sense of empowerment. She began to alert me when she thought I should begin to take notes. When I once asked her in response, how she was able to determine that she was about to speak schizophrenese, she replied, 'It's when I put things together in strange ways that no-one else would understand,' adding, 'I take a giant leap.' Here are two examples. My comments and questions to her are interpolated in brackets.

Caroline had gone to play pool after taking her car to be repaired. It had been damaged due to her usual irresponsible driving:

I had time to kill. Rack it up and pocket 'em. Sock it and rock 'em. Clear the table. The only table that had monkey business to it. [?] E. [a staff member in the hospital, whom Caroline idealized] and I used to play pool. [?] Judgement Day. I've got so many balls and I have to put them in the pocket. Get the eight-ball in and you're out. I've got to shoot straight from the hip and keep both feet on the ground. Just straight shots coming from the heart. People have things racked up against you, but you keep on shooting, and if you make a racket like me it gives them more ammunition. [?] Now you *really* think I'm crazy. I racked 'em up and then I bought a root beer. The guy said, 'You can't drink that here', and then we talked about getting 50% off lodging in [a distant resort]. I said that late September is the best time to go there [laughs]. [*What are you laughing about?*] Well, it's not a short walk to get there, and I have $16 in my wallet. They don't want unethical behaviour in the bar. So, I think about going there; I build up in my mind places to go. I start out thinking I'm going to clean the apartment. Then I do these other things. Then I start thinking when I don't that it's the fault of the landlord and others. Then I ran out of time, and I had to go to work; I was late again. [*What about the resort?*] It's a *Closetland* place [a reference to a movie about a woman who turned to fantasy in order to endure torture]; no problems there, everything is fine.

The structural difference between neurosis and psychosis **81**

Caroline begins by trying to tell me something in the language of primordial mentation. Suddenly she reflects that I will think she is crazy. At first, she tries to explain her thought process in more primordial language, but gradually she makes a transition into reflective thought that is less concrete and enactive and more symbolic. She is not entirely successful but here is what I am able to reconstruct:

> The Day of Judgement has come for me. I'm in a rage at myself for all my monkey business—damaging my car, not being financially responsible, not cleaning my apartment or being on time for my work and treating life like a game in which the object is to lose. I give others ammunition to use against me. I've really got myself behind the eight-ball and I've got to get my feet back on the ground. But I'm in a rage at having to be responsible; I just want to kill more time, blame others, wipe the table clean of all my problems and imagine I'm at a resort on a perpetual vacation.

Here is another example:

> I walked around the lake with my mother when my affair with my college professor was going on [perhaps 15 years previously] and tried to tell her about it. So, the last few days I found three lakes and walked around them. Three guys were on one dock. Things reminded me of the professor. Birds on an island in the first lake remind me of a man who didn't disclose that he was probably having other relationships—probably screwing other women, all those birds—but it was hard to keep my mind together walking around the big lake because it was so big; too big a place to keep my mind. Then these guys started flirting, playing with my mind. All three of those lakes make a penis; the end, the middle, the part you play with. [*Why did you decide to take the walk?*] I did it so I could focus on a destructive relationship; I was trying to feel the feeling I once had with my mother after the affair. But the lakes are such a big temptation to fall in it again. Walking around the smaller lake I could get more in touch with the feeling of loss and hurt, some of the feeling; but it wasn't satisfying. The bigger lakes were overwhelming, and I didn't know why I was there anymore; I was trying to get into trouble. The birds on the big lake felt threatening; all the people he screwed; the things I didn't see. I was foolish; I start to realise it but then instead it becomes my mother fooled me, not what I did. My mother goes to [her winter vacation home] and spends time watching the birds. I feel betrayed. I went to the dock and saw two birds in a caged area; I felt caged. I wondered if those women were prostitutes and ended in jail. [?] I'm trying to deal with what happened in my twenties with the professor. Around the lake my mother and I walked, and I told her. [Her mother had blamed the professor and told Caroline not to worry about what she had done.] The lie was talking to my mother about

82 The structural difference between neurosis and psychosis

it and my mother's lies. My interest in the lake is a re-creation of the crime when something equals nothing, and nothing equals something. The lively pond is a metaphor for my mind, and my difficulty containing limits and boundaries; staying in bounds and not destroying everything; attending to a straight line of thought. The kids represent how easily I'm distracted and take my mind off. The lake is a reference to my mind, and the tree is my interest in life. The tree and the birds are a blaming thing. People don't tell others about their affairs, but they communicate inside themselves about it. My mind is the pond, the tree. Claustrophobia is how 'in the dark' a part of me is. My thoughts versus my actions. I say one thing, make my pledges, then I go do another. Destructive. I'm terrified of the temptation to blow everything to bits. My tree is empty and alone; others have things in their branches. I can't walk a straight line; I veer off, so I try another planet. It's painful. I know if I can't stay on line in this little pond then I'll never get anywhere in the bigger issues in life; I can look at trees that seem more interesting, but I have to be able to deal with what's here. [*Now you are speaking in metaphor; why don't you always?*] Metaphors take more responsibility; they are more connecting.

Sara

Unfortunately, I have had to omit most of the strange and exciting elements in Sara's 11-year therapy in order to focus on the transition she made between the primordial mental organization underlying psychosis to a neurotic organization based on reflective representational thought. This transition enabled her to move from a disabled state that would most certainly have ended in her death, and a diagnosis of chronic paranoid schizophrenia, to a meaningful life of creativity and relationships. A more complete summary of our work can be found in my 2019 book.

Sara had been hospitalized intermittently with increasing frequency and duration since mid-adolescence in the more than a decade preceding my first encounter with her in her late 20s, and she was becoming increasingly destructive to herself. She had been hospitalized again with the diagnosis of chronic paranoid schizophrenia and told that if she could find a therapist who would be responsible for her, she could be discharged. A friend called me to make an appointment as Sara was too terrified to do it. During our first meeting Sara told me was that her problem was inability to concentrate and lack of a sense of personal identity. As we talked, she reported a sensation that the top of her head was lifting off and she said she was hearing voices that were harassing and frightening her. In other words, she was functioning in an undifferentiated unintegrated primordial cosmos dominated by self-destructive rage, in which, as she said, there was no cohesive sense of self or differentiation of separate others.

Sara typically sat near the door with her head averted, with her coat on and purse clutched to her lap; and she often bolted out the door a few

The structural difference between neurosis and psychosis **83**

minutes early. There were long silences sometimes punctuated with sotto voce mocking laughter or muttered curses or gibberish about shapes and patterns. She believed bombs were planted in the walls and planes and missiles were about to attack and kill her. Our sessions consisted of a curious triadic relationship among Sara, myself, and a Greek chorus of female voices that terrorized her as they instructed her how to cope with the dangerous world she was in and threatened to punish her if she related to me because I was trying to kill her.

As our meetings continued, she told me that in her previous extensive contacts with psychiatrists she believed she had acted crazy because that was what was they expected of her. She was contemptuous of them because she believed she was successful in fooling them. She soon became frustrated with me because she felt that unlike others, I gave her little clue about what I wanted from her. After some months, she began to make brief eye contact and express moments of feeling manifest by incipient tears and wishes to "scream bloody murder" and kill everyone. At such times her thoughts short-circuited, and she often bolted from the office. This was the beginning of a long slow process of emotional integration and awareness.

After some months, Sara reluctantly admitted she was beginning to like me, and with the lack of awareness of contradiction characteristic of primordial mentation said that for this reason she said she wanted to shoot and kill me. Enactment rather than reflection is another characteristic of this process, and she began to miss sessions and travel to places where she would get herself into situations in which she was severely abused, and her life was in danger. She wanted to purchase a gun and kill me. At the same time, she was afraid that I might die. But if I did it would be a relief, for then she could go to a gambling establishment, lose all her savings, purchase a gun, and kill herself. She was still in the throes of lack of integration and impulsive enactment.

One day she informed me that she had never hallucinated or been ill, and the stories she had been telling me were manifestations of her ability to fool and manipulate people, especially "shrinks" for whom she had great contempt. In retrospect, I suppose she had intuited in her own strange way that I wanted her to get better and was giving me what would please me. She talked about her difficulty letting herself depend on anyone. I felt both pleased at her seeming sanity and deeply unsettled and confused about the abrupt transition, which made no sense. But this oasis was brief, and soon she wondered if the wiring in my office was connected to explosives, if I had a gun in my drawer, and if I was about to strangle her. She began frequenting bars where she would get drunk and invite abuse. When she said she planned to go to a distant city, I arranged for her to be hospitalized, where she remained for the next 1 1/2 years. She barricaded herself in her hospital room, and in a state of terror that staff were trying to kill her she assaulted them and had to be put in seclusion and sometimes restraints, which only served to confirm her beliefs.

84 The structural difference between neurosis and psychosis

She would huddle in corners, grimace and make strange body movements, bang her head against the wall, twist and smash her hands violently, glance around the room apprehensively and pick at her face. She experienced visual hallucinations of fragmented floating body parts and voices threatening her with terrifying scenarios or "protecting" her from harm by commanding that she act in ways that were self-destructive.

Between meetings she wrote me a remarkable letter indicating more mature emotional awareness. Throughout much of our relationship she wrote me letters that indicated much more emotional awareness than she was able to articulate when she sat with me:

> I really think I am alive, and if I think about it, I get so sad and I get really angry. When I sit in the room with you, and I let myself believe you are there I feel so safe I just want to sit there forever. But I can't seem to be able to believe it for very long afterwards. I had no idea what I was getting into by entering therapy and I'm scared, and I do hate you, but I also wish I could be with you every minute.

Over the ensuing weekend Sara briefly escaped from the hospital in near zero temperature, without a coat.

At the beginning of our second year, she gave me a self-portrait. In addition to revealing her considerable artistic ability what was striking was that it looked like an aerial view of a landscape consisting of geometric plots each filled with busy designs and a large empty space in the middle, that I understood as a graphic depiction of the absence of an integrated self and the chaos of undifferentiated externalized hostility.

Sara's capacity to seem rational and logical based on paranoid manipulation of what she imagined to be a hostile dangerous world was very effective in convincing hospital staff that she was normal and simply feigning illness, and that it was me and my "therapy" that was driving her crazy. She covertly enlisted otherwise well-intentioned staff in an attempt to get me removed from her case by convincing them I was harming her and making her worse.

Sara began for the first time to note the passage of time in relation to the rhythm of our scheduled appointments. She worried about my forthcoming summer vacation. This was one of the beginnings of the long transition to the second mental structure and reflective representational thought. However, when I left, she escaped and bought a plane ticket to Europe. At the last minute, she changed her mind and returned to the hospital where she got sexually involved with a male patient who was known for his violent behavior. She sent a letter to me that said, in part:

> I am really lost; I am 1,000,000 miles away and I don't know where that is. I have all these fantasies about taking off with him, staying stoned, drunk,

getting pimped out, beaten up. I want to cry and scream and hit people and I am so angry. You know I am really smart. I am creative and imaginative I could've done a hell of a lot with myself, and here I am coming up on 30 and I am sitting in a nut house kissing a fucking psychopath. I am so angry at you. I want to scream, tear the room apart.

When I returned from my summer vacation, Sara said that she was enraged that I had left her but that it had not been safe for her to leave me in retaliation until I returned. She then lost control and when restrained and placed in the quiet room she giggled, hallucinated, and banged her head against the wall.

Late in our second year, emotional awareness of sadness, anger, and a sense of the passage of time and related childhood memories began to surface with regularly. Sara looked forward to her hours with me and reported a feeling of security she claimed was entirely novel in her life. She told me this was the first experience in her life of a caring relationship with another person in which her needs were satisfied and the realization made her depressed and enraged. In other words, caring was a chink in her armor and a threat to her "independence."

Sara was again confined to the quiet room because she had begun to tear at the skin on her face in what she admitted was an effort to tear her face off. I shared with her my feelings of powerlessness to help her, and we both marveled at the power of her hatred. She regained some self-control and became very sad as she realized her drive to destroy what was important to her. She realized that she was trying to drive me crazy.

After more than two years of therapy and a year and a half of hospitalization Sara moved to a halfway house. She realized the hospital had become a kind of home and family.

Further transition to reflective thought was manifest in the fact she was able to begin studies toward a master's degree in teaching. There were episodes of caring and therapeutic insight, but these alternated with reversions to primordial mental activity consisting of paranoid detachment and lengthy silence, and I found myself responding with sleepiness and boredom to the rhythmic alternation between the two structural processes. When she noticed this, Sara articulated wishes to tease and torture me and put me in a dark place so that I would feel trapped and alone, and give up hope as she was forced to do as a child, detach myself from my body and feelings and go crazy. She was relieved next hour to find I was still intact.

Sara told me life was becoming meaningful to her, that she was taking better care of herself, and she expressed gratitude. She felt pain immediately when she accidentally jabbed her hand on a nail head, the beginning integration of a body-self. For the first time in her life, she took a stuffed animal to bed with her.

In our fourth year of work, Sara struggled with feelings of homelessness and wishes to be my little child, on the one hand; and on the other, terror of me because I looked crazy, that she associated with the urge to speed, get picked up by the police, attack them and get killed. Eventually she sought help of the staff at the halfway house and was briefly and constructively re-hospitalized. She said, "if I'm going to feel all this stuff then I want to have people around all the time to share it with." The struggle with reflective emotional thought alternated with primordial mentation but then, and for a long time to come she was not able to experience caring and hatred as aspects of an intrapsychic conflict, so the states were enacted. She wished to go to a foreign country where she did not speak the language so there could be no communication. I commented that that country was called the land of backward schizophrenia. Sara moved out of the halfway house and into a house she rented jointly with several women. At night when she began to be terrified and paranoid she hugged her stuffed animal, expressing increasing cohesion of self.

Sara began practice teaching and also began to keep a diary between sessions in the in the form of letters to me. She wrote:

> I would like to kill a lot of people and they don't know it but really I don't want to kill you. I wish I could give you a big hug and tell you how I feel, that I am so lonely and so tired and so scared and I can't sleep. I know it won't be you that kills me, it is my feelings that I think will kill me; feeling good, safe, loving you, wanting to hug you and never leave. I think of you sitting in your chair and I feel warm inside and safe and so sad I can hardly bear it, like I could cry forever.

She was beginning to integrate her emotional life and to realize that the attacks came from within her, to represent internal awareness of a love-hate conflict.

She decided that she needed to talk with me about sex since she wanted to have children of her own, and she was beginning to show some interest in men. This marked the beginnings of a transition from mindless enactment to reflective thought; and it involved separation of immediate experience from memory, the beginnings of a sense of future and of past, and becoming more self-directed. She realized she had transformed passive enactments in which she put herself in situations of harm into omnipotent beliefs she was controlling men, by being unaware of her own emotions.

In our fifth year of work, her sense of time continued to expand, and she began to envision a future and for the first time feel hopeful. She was doing very well at school, but she fought with me over everything. She received her Master's degree and at graduation fellow students and teachers expressed caring for her and described her as gifted and creative. She told me that for the first time in her life she felt optimistic and excited and had even purchased a dress to wear to a job interview. She was certain she now had enough control so that she would not become psychotic during our upcoming summer separation. At the conclusion of the last hour, she shook my hand, expressed her gratitude to me for having "put up" with her and said she would miss me.

When we resumed in the fall, Sara was less rigid physically and emotionally, and more spontaneous. She was more sensitive to temperature and pain, indicating more caring integration of her body. She sat a bit closer to me in the room, spontaneously clapped her hands when she said something, and wanted to examine an object of interest in my office. At times she sat back and relaxed, and once yelled in an angry voice, "fuck you." These gestures and spontaneous expressions of emotion terrified her.

For the first time she began to worry about real problems of her life like finding a caring husband, rather than about her hallucinations and delusions. She realized that she wanted to have children and that there were now men she liked. When her first teaching year ended during the sixth year of our work, students, their parents, and faculty praised her and expressed their gratitude. Sara planned a holiday trip abroad with a friend. She gave me a small gift before leaving and shook my hand, demonstrating a violent physical oscillation I now associated with alternating holding on and breaking off; love and hate; enactment and reflection. At the beginning of our separation Sara had the first dream that she could recall in which I figured, which she told me on her return. This was further indication of growing positive mental representation of my presence in her life. She wrote me another letter indicating further differentiation of past and present and integration of her emotions. It read, in part: "It is becoming clear what I want and what I don't want, and I didn't get, and that clarity makes me so angry it scares the hell out of me."

When we met in the fall Sara told me how constructive her month had been. She had purchased a house of her own in a safe neighborhood, was being assertive and creative at work, and had maintained a sense of me within her that helped her make good decisions. As usual there was another side that she had to enact as she was still unable to fully represent and reflect upon internal conflict. She began to miss appointments and then reported a dream in which she had spilled coffee on the lovely dining table she had purchased for her new home, and in order to avoid awareness of the contrast between the marred area and the rest of the tabletop she hacked it to pieces. The dream reflected a further step toward internal experience of conflict over love and hate.

Sara told me she was afraid she might wear two mismatched shoes to a forthcoming parent's meeting, and she realized this represented how little dialogue there was between the caring and hating parts of herself. I suggested that she try to find names for each one and that she sit in different chairs in the office when talking from each position. She called the two parts "black" and "red" and over the next five weeks we elaborated the characteristics of each.

88 The structural difference between neurosis and psychosis

At the conclusion of this hour she said, quite unaware, "I'm going to take care of myself even if it kills me!"

In our seventh year, she had a dream in which I appeared, and was dismayed to acknowledge that it indicated my importance but also the limitations she maintained. We were sleeping in separate sleeping bags, each entirely zipped up, on a beach on the northern coast. We had been there a long time, there was water and a line of seaweed over much of us, and she was half awake. This clear illustration of our disengagement and the endless deadening of our relationship distressed her. She admitted that she missed me and had pretended the teddy bear she now used for comfort represented me, but then, reverting from integration to paranoid disintegration, she called herself a "stupid jerk." She told me she had made a new female friend, had joined a health club and was expressing anger more appropriately when people mistreated her. At the end of this hour of struggle to integrate and heal she reported "a splitting headache."

I have not described her long and inconsistent history about medication, in which for the most part she either did not take what was prescribed but kept the fact secret, or else fought against its effects. Now she agreed with my suggestion that she resume trifluoperazine in a way that indicated a change in attitude. Almost immediately her hallucinations diminished, and she became calmer and better able to sleep, to focus attention and concentrate and organize her life. She recalled her struggles in the hospital to fight off the effects of medication and felt terrified that she was allowing someone (her words) to get into her mouth and influence her. We were able to work together, as one would with a neurotic person capable of reflection and the experience of conflict, on her rage at "swallowing" anything, initially somatic related to plausible reconstruction of her breast-feeding experiences with a mother who seemingly hated her, then memories of performing fellatio, and finally the problems she had with me related to the taking in involved with learning.

Sara described a dream:

I was searching for something but there was this demon following me around in the shadows killing people. It was like some robot that ripped the tops of people's heads off and ate their brains and hands. It killed everyone that I saw or talked to. What a vivid picture of what I am doing! The monster is obviously me and I can't kill it and you can't kill it because all it does is constantly tried to kill you. I don't think you really understand what a monster I am. I get you where it hurts. I get you to care about me and try to help and then kick you in the head over and over.

She reported a "splitting headache" as she contemplated the part of her that wanted to be close to people and the part that was enraged at human beings.

The structural difference between neurosis and psychosis **89**

In our ninth year, she missed many appointments and during her sessions made the tape recorder, which we had long ago agreed she should use and usually did constructively, malfunction. She picked fights with me over everything and came close to ending her therapy. She left a session only to discover that she had locked herself out of her car, and she had to return to the office for help. The next hour, after characteristic preliminary cursing, she said she had been relieved to find herself locked out of her car because she was certain that had been her unconscious effort to keep herself from driving off and ending our relationship, and this was the first instance she could recall in which her unconscious motivation had been constructive!

This was a clear indication of work toward conflict resolution. Unlike other positive moments in our work this incident heralded a permanent change. Sara no longer seemed psychotic. She told me that to her surprise she had never been this depressed before without having delusions and hallucinations. Klein would call this the depressive position in which paranoid-schizoid disintegration and undifferentiation are transformed into an internal sense of self and reflective thought. Sara decided to cut the frequency of our therapy to once weekly. We met for another year and a half prior to terminating and there was no recurrence of hallucinations or delusions. Sara reported progressive expansion in the areas of close friendships and work. She began to develop an identity as an educational crusader as evidenced by meteoric career advancement and the high esteem in which she was held by other educators, parents, and most of all the children she taught. It became clear that the extent of her professional ambition and effort would be the only limiting factor in the success of her career.

She still wrote occasional letters. In another she wrote: "You have also, like you said a long time ago, given me choices. My happiness with what I have now fuels my rage and urge to destroy you and my feelings, destroy myself. But much of me wants more and thinks that I can go further."

We agreed to her wish to end scheduled appointments and to visit and report to me every half year or so, in the hope that eventually she might be able to reach a more internally consistent decision about her therapy and herself. During one such interval she wrote me:

There are nights when I get so depressed and feel helpless and angry and want to die, but I can survive them, I have control and know more clearly that the feelings will not kill me. I do not take drastic action anymore. Often, I don't pay attention to my feelings, and it is only when I get very close to being psychotic that I force myself to figure out what is going on. You helped me to do this many, many times. I can do it myself now. Thank you for your patience and caring. Thank you for giving me choices. You sat there for years waiting for me to show up. You ran the risk of holding out your caring and being rejected over and over and over. I know that I didn't entirely arrive, but I am happy. I know that it is not ideal that I carry you around in my head as a watchdog. Ideally it should be me that does this but the part of me that wants to destroy all caring and all life is very powerful, and I need you there in my mind as a third-party.

Because the man she loved lived and worked in a distant city and she needed to get a PhD in order to advance further in her work, they decided to get married, and she decided to end her therapy and move. She came to see me for a couple final appointments and said goodbye with tears and heartfelt expressions of gratitude.

Years elapsed without any word from Sara. After about 20 years, I received a call from her saying she was travelling through the part of the country where my office is located and wondered if she could visit.

I felt I was in the presence of an impressively mature woman with a solid sense of self who made direct eye and emotional contact with me, had a sense of values and purpose, and was highly intelligent and articulate. She described a very satisfying marriage. She and her husband had adopted a disturbed adolescent boy and raised him to a constructive and mature manhood. She had concluded an outstanding career as teacher and educational innovator and decided to get a master's degree in creative writing and become an author. She had never again sought or required therapy or medication. What she recalled most about our work was my unwavering patience and caring during her long periods of hostility and disengagement. I have since discovered that she wrote two young adult novels that received excellent national reviews. As I discovered reading them subsequently, their settings and themes clearly related to her own struggles as an adolescent.

12

MENTAL STRUCTURE, SOCIAL ORGANIZATION, AND THE COMPLEX INTERPLAY OF SOCIALLY CONSTRUCTIVE AND DESTRUCTIVE PHENOMENA ARISING FROM THEM

The generally accepted wisdom is that the human species is superior to others because it has created culture and civilization, beyond the capacity of other animals that are thought of as uncivilized and destructively aggressive, even if we may longer believe they are savages. However, E. O. Wilson demonstrated in his sociobiological model that destructiveness in socio-centric species that do not develop a second mental structure is for the most part limited to the constructive function of equilibration and survival of the social group and the species within ordinarily expectable environmental conditions. In other words, it has a positive regulatory function. The human species is not so constructive and there is much evidence to suggest that human destructiveness does not serve the social and species constructive role it does in other species.

Human infants whose navigation of the phases of attachment and separation is secure develop a second mental structure in the course of maturation, and as a result of it acquire the capacity for selective adaptive choice between primordial and thoughtful mentation both in individual expression and in formation of groups. These new group formations include both families and larger social structures organized primarily around belief systems and ones organized around individual initiative and creativity. These groups, in turn, can function in harmony or in potentially destructive conflict with other groups of similar origin. Infants who do not successfully negotiate the attachment-separation phase become maladapted adults, destructive to themselves and to society. The effect of the uniquely human acquisition of a second mental structure, or of the failure to achieve it in the process of development, is that the role of social destructiveness is no longer simply homeostasis and enhancement of group and species survival, but may function in ways both

DOI: 10.4324/9781003435785-12

92 The complex interplay of structure and destruction

socially destructive and antithetical to the long-term welfare of the species. This chapter describes some of these.

Social groupings formed by individuals by sharing a primordial mental structure are otherwise known as belief systems, and they can be constructive or destructive of themselves and in relation to the broader society of which they are a part. Many are basically peaceful and harmonious, though insular in relation to the larger society. They discourage contact with new ideas and discourage reflective thought as part of child development. Education designed to help children to learn to think for themselves, science and medicine are threatening to beliefs that are often couched in religious terms. Parents and children in such groups have loving relationships so long as there is no individual deviation from the beliefs that unite them. As for the organizations themselves, so long as they are not disturbed by outside influences based on reflective thought and its consequences, all remains well. They are conservative in the sense of being predicated on conformity, and do not promote development of a self that is organized around reflective thought and respect for individual differences. Social destructiveness occurs when members of such groups become exposed to reflective thought and ideas that are different. The 1925 trial *The State of Tennessee v. John Thomas Scopes* described later in the chapter illustrates such a collision of thought and belief.

Social systems based on the primordial structure can be destructive of themselves; cults are the most malignant example. Cults are systems comprised of two types of persons that are mutually dependent, who act as complementary parts of a primordially structured system: passive, compliant followers and an active pontifical leader. They combine to form an undifferentiated identity whose extreme destructive beliefs are manifestly delusional. They license and encourage violent expression of unintegrated, undifferentiated, uncontrolled rage. Neither of the component part-personalities is able to develop and sustain an integrated cohesive internal mind and to separate and live without the other. As a single entity they are unable to experience, reflect upon and control emotions, particularly fear and rage. Cults collude in promoting enactment of elements that they are unable to own as cohesive selves. The members tend to be paranoid and attribute the rage and malevolent intentions they are unaware of within themselves to others. Examples include Charles Manson and his followers, who murdered prominent celebrities in 1969 based on the belief they were evil and harbored murderous intentions toward members of the cult, and the Branch Davidian cult directed by David Koresh who engaged in a violent confrontation with authority in Waco Texas in 1993. The leader foments the followers to enact his unintegrated rage toward others who are misperceived to be the bearers of the malignant intentions. The Westboro Baptist Church in Topeka, Kansas, under the leadership of Fred Phelps, is a more recent example. It is organized around enactment of hatred toward homosexuals, veterans, and others who have been victims

The complex interplay of structure and destruction   **93**

of catastrophes; based on religiously framed beliefs by Phelps and his wife that such persons have violated God's laws. The catastrophes these people have experienced are understood as part of their just punishment by God, and using righteous quotations from Biblical scripture, the cult casts itself as God's instrument; chosen to be His punitive hand. Cults are small because they appeal to the most severely psychotic person in the population.

Larger organizations based on shared primordial mentation can be found among national governments and major religions as well. Religions are comprised of shared belief systems or ideologies. Nations can be loosely grouped as democratic, autocratic, or fascist. However, recent social awareness in the United States has raised the possibility that our democracy may be a fictional ideal, as the so-called democracy Americans have wanted to believe they enjoy seems to have been based on shared beliefs (not susceptible to reason) about White Christian male supremacy, and related socially sanctioned hostility toward and disenfranchisement of those who do not fit those categories.

The penchant for ideologically based violence that characterizes religious extremism – such as the Inquisition, the Crusades, Jihad – is a kind of fascism. But although religions are organized around systematic attribution of hostile evil intentions to non-believers, the majority of humans accept religious belief as a normal, even essential, aspect of life; remain capable of functioning according to reflective thought for the most part; and except in more extreme instances, consider persons outside the pale simply as other, or as unenlightened, rather than as undifferentiated receptacles for hostile intentions. These beliefs appear to be more ritualistic than enactive.

The demarcation between autocracy or dictatorship and fascism is not clear-cut. In general, it has to do with the presence or absence of shared ideology. A population that shares feelings of deprivation and resentment is ripe for a fascist leader. Leaders like Hitler gain power because their ideology of racial or ethnic purification and privilege appeals to a wider spectrum of people than does that of a cult, which tends to attract persons who are psychotic. Followers feel entitled to "legally" express rage toward those identified as responsible for their real or imagined deprivation and to believe that in so doing they will achieve an ideal state of well-being.

Dictatorship involves undifferentiation of leader from follower that is based more on fear than on wishful entitlement. Rather than appealing to delusions that an ideal self can be had by licensing personal expression of hostility and appealing to hopes for restitution, dictatorships require and enforce subjugation of self by instilling and enforcing terror on those who deviate and might have the temerity to question the leader. The ideological othering element – encouraging members to enact hatred toward and suspiciousness of groups of people identified as "other" – is directed toward members of the group who might show signs of deviation. Dictatorships are more common in less developed countries whose citizens have traditionally been anonymous mistreated

94 The complex interplay of structure and destruction

cogs in a larger machine and who have not developed the refined sense of individual rights and entitlement characteristic of contemporary Western societies.

Of course, not all those who allow themselves to be subjugated by dictators and fascist leaders are psychotic. People who are not sufficiently secure to risk autonomous difference with powerful leaders are susceptible to the influence of leaders who not only threaten autonomous expression of difference but give permission for and reward regressive expression of fear and rage.

The results of the presidential elections first of Donald Trump and then of Joseph Biden have left many educated observers shocked to discover the large proportion of the population who support Trump and echo and promulgate his grandiose delusional beliefs and his leadership style that combines elements of fascism and dictatorship. The idea that half the population of a nation is psychotic is inconsistent with ordinary understanding of the concept of normality and deviance, which is based on social consensus. To understand this tsunami of support it is first necessary to realize that several different kinds of persons may use primordial mental activity, and then to understand the special circumstances in which their interests align so that they act synergistically.

One such group consists of persons who have been unable to form a stable attachment to a primary caregiver and develop a separate sense of self. These are the individuals who fit the description of psychosis. They are particularly susceptible to involvement in movements that offer them a home in the sense of support for their beliefs and actions.

Another group is comprised of members of orthodox social enclaves based on a particular kind of caring that is restricted to others who share a common belief system that is xenophobic, and views anyone with a different opinion or way of thinking as enemy and dangerous. One example of this behavior is the 1925 Scopes "Monkey Trial", which was the basis for the 1960 movie *Inherit the Wind*. As with many such groups, it was ordinarily peaceful until galvanized to destructive action by external incendiary influences. The agenda of the ACLU in 1925 was an example of one such force, and the more recent influence of the Trump movement is another.

The ACLU, in its infancy in 1925, decided to challenge the anti-scientific pro-religious Tennessee law prohibiting teaching of evolution in the schools. The lawsuit led members of the Dayton, Tennessee community to believe they could gain national recognition of their beliefs by serving as a test case for the importance of Creationism. They enlisted John T. Scopes, a substitute teacher who was not sure he had ever actually taught the scientific theory of evolution, to challenge the law. They hired the well-known attorney Clarence Darrow and enlisted William Jennings Bryan, a deeply religious man who repudiated science, to represent the community. The result was the

The complex interplay of structure and destruction **95**

conversion of an otherwise more or less satisfied peaceful community into an inflamed destructive mob, aroused to hatred and violence.

Representative Marjorie Taylor Greene, who was chosen to represent a Republican enclave in rural Georgia near Appalachia during the Biden election, is a more recent example. Members of the tightly knit community she came to represent are xenophobic, but as they all agree with one another they had no need to search for an enemy on which to enact their hatred. Greene, however, mobilized this community into action, espousing expression of hatred of Muslims, Jews, non-whites: anyone different from herself. She embraced conspiracy theories including the delusion that wealthy Jews using lasers from outer space were responsible for California wildfires. She denied that events, like the 9/11 destruction of the twin towers and some of the massive school shootings, actually occurred. And she supported Donald Trump's delusion that he had won the presidential election and the presidency had been stolen from him. When interviewed subsequent to her election some members of the rural farming community that elected her expressed surprise and embarrassment about the extreme expression of her views, but continued to support her basic positions, because the shared beliefs underlying them had unified their community for decades and held the promise of spreading their beliefs.

Other persons in the destructive coalition that supports Trump have been able to develop some sense of separate self and reflective thought but retain islands of primordial mental activity because of fundamental insecurity. These people are vulnerable to regression and are susceptible to the kind of "home" that shared belief systems and the temptation to support violence might offer. Many of the Republicans who privately express reservations about Trump, but publicly stand behind him out of fear of retaliation or loss of their positions of power, seem to belong to this group.

Finally, some persons who operate from reflective thought but have a limited moral sense might exploit the extremism of these others for their own political purposes. The former Vice President Pence and the former majority leader of the Senate Mitch McConnell may fit this latter politicly opportunistic category.

The catalyst for this coalition and conflagration seems to have been the charismatic leadership of Donald Trump, whose socially successful primordial mental functioning appears to have been the result of an extraordinary adjustment to extreme trauma and insecurity in the infantile stage of attachment and separation; leading to development of the ability to control others and gain their unequivocal support. He provided the match that lit the incendiary explosive coalition of destructive forces: the coming together of psychotic persons, of large social groups organized around primordial mental activity, of persons susceptible to regression when offered a primordial belief "home," and opportunists who operated from reflective

96 The complex interplay of structure and destruction

thought but exploited the growing movement for their own power-seeking purposes.

This eruption of human destructiveness is but the latest episode of a clash that has occurred repeatedly since social organizations first emerged in the Middle Ages based on individual self-actualization, rather than the traditional ones in which persons were cogs in a larger social entity, and destructiveness served the function of group homeostasis and species survival regardless of its effect on individual members. The subsequent iterations of this clash have pitted bastions of education and science, humanistic social organizations, and those who attempt to form governments based on reflective thought and respectful awareness of individual differences and rights, against organizations based on the fundamental hate-driven premise that only a single point of view and its advocates can exist.

In its most recent American political incarnation, it has led to ongoing debate about whether this difference can be addressed and resolved by encouraging rational dialogue between members of opposing groups: the saying has been "across the aisle." Persons steeped in the mental structure of reflective thought want to believe that the representatives of each point of view can somehow achieve harmony and consensus because the difference is one of social and economic issues. They fail to understand that the clash is much more fundamental, between groups formed and dependent on two different and antithetical mental structures. I think it safe to say that the core of the chasm relates to the fact that the factions represent qualitatively different, immiscible mental structures and their expression. One supports the principle of awareness and respect for individual difference, self-control, and reflective efforts to determine what is real and true, whereas the other is based on fixed belief and conformity to a non-rational system. The first involves curiosity and a search for truth and reality, the second begins with the conviction that wisdom has been received and individual curiosity and questioning is to be suppressed. The first is based on caring for others, whether or not they think as we do, so long as they do not do tangible harm whereas the second equates caring with agreement, and views difference and disagreement as inherently dangerous and evil.

For this reason, communication between representatives of the two forms of mental activity is most likely impossible. The inevitable result is struggle for dominance, in which representatives of primordial mentation attempt to subdue, convert, or exterminate those who disagree, whereas representatives of reflective thought try to educate, and when that fails, fight to contain and control those who believe otherwise.

Another class of social conflict will get just brief mention before concluding the discussion about how the human difference, the acquisition of a second mental structure, has led to new and heterogeneous social organizations some of which are internally destructive, and many that are antagonistic to one another. Social conflict occurs among groups organized about different conclusions majorities of their memberships may reach based on reflective thought. This is mature conflict, based on developed individual selves who might see "data" in the world around them differently, and is usually, but not always, conducted harmoniously albeit passionately.

13

MENTAL STRUCTURES AND THE EVOLUTION OF HOMO SAPIENS

The human mind is unique among species. In addition to the biologically determined structure present at birth, humans normally acquire a second structure, reflective representational thought. The process of evolution that has brought this about, its development in individual humans, its manifestations, and its implications for the future of our species, has been the subject of the book.

The prevalent psychoanalytic understanding about mental structure remains based on Freud's theory that mind is comprised of three structures, "an" id, ego, and superego, whose dynamic interactional complexities are fueled by two mental drives, which in turn somehow arise from biological instincts common to all animals. This assumption continues to exert a powerful hold on devotees of classical psychoanalytic theory despite decades of doubt about its validity and utility. Freud did not attempt to explain why humans develop mental structures that other animals do not have, or how homo sapiens made the leap he inferred from biological instinct to psychological structure. He advanced other related incorrect beliefs as well, including that all species share a common biological origin, and that destructiveness in humans is similar in origin and function to that of other species. Freud's proposed mental structures are based on his limited knowledge of sociology, cultural anthropology, and evolutionary science, all of which originated around or not long before he created psychoanalysis. He believed that the authoritarian social structure of nineteenth-century Viennese society was common to all social structure. The developmental schema he based upon that assumption, and the model of psychopathology (neurosis) based on it, is based on the assumption that infants must subordinate individual drive-wishes to the will of social authority (the Oedipus complex and threat of castration) in order for

DOI: 10.4324/9781003435785-13

Mental structures and the evolution of homo sapiens **99**

civilization to exist. It does not account for the fundamental developmental role of the earlier stage of attachment and separation, or for the role of mothers, or for the psychoses. This book has addressed these problems.

The biology of neoteny that distinguishes humans from other species has necessitated complex learning from caregivers and the environment that distinguishes humans from other species. A consequence of this learning is the acquisition of a second mental structure. What makes humans unique – development of a second mental structure – introduces multiple complexities of individual behavior and social organization that expand beyond simple arithmetical summation, especially as, for many people, the transition either never occurs or is incomplete. This creates opportunities and problems for humans that are not in the cosmos of other species.

One of these is that humans speak two languages, and if we are mature, we can move between one and the other adaptively as personal and social circumstances dictate. The first of these is biologically programmed and present at birth, and the second language is learned more or less completely depending on caregivers and on how we transit the early stages of attachment and separation. This language complexity is not equivalent to learning a second language in addition to the one that is common to the geographic region and culture into which we are born. In fact, the fluency and semantic maturity with which that kind of second language is learned depends on how early in the attachment-separation phase learning of the second language occurs, and how successful development of the second language is. Unfortunately, the predominant model in linguistics is that reflective thought evolves directly from a biological process Noam Chomsky and associates called universal grammar. It is based on the incorrect assumption that all languages have the capacity for reflective thought, or recursion. Such a definition excludes the communication of infants and small children based on the primordial structure (Robbins, 2018a, 2018b), and it is one Freud believed as well, as he equated the primary process with unconsciousness – so that it follows infants and small children are unconscious!

All animals are conscious and intelligent. Intelligence arising from the primary mental structure is common to all animals including humans. Failure to recognize this has led to the protest movement of recent decades intended to demonstrate how intelligent members of other species are. Moreover, that same structure underlies many normal and creative states in adult life such as parenting, creativity, and religious belief. It is the foundation for social organizations based on maintenance of the integrity and equilibrium of the organization, rather than the individuality of its members. These include ones we consider normal, like religions and conservative political movements; and others we consider pathological like cults, fascism, and delusional frenzies such as the Inquisition and the Salem witchcraft trials.

100 Mental structures and the evolution of homo sapiens

The attachment-separation phase is the great divide in the structuring of mind and in human development. It is the watershed that separates neurotic from psychotic pathology.

The applicability of Freud's model of psychopathology, neurosis, is limited to a later stage of development as it assumes a mind based upon the second mental structure, reflective representational thought, that is integrated, differentiated, and capable of relating to a separate person (the analyst) and experiencing and exploring intrapsychic conflict. It does not explain why and how humans uniquely develop such a structure, nor does it account for psychotic pathology based on the primordial structure in which there is no coherent integrated sense of self and no ability to differentiate a separate helping other. Freud's beliefs about the mind were based on an incomplete understanding of his own personality, and an understanding of social organization limited both by that and by his overgeneralization of the paternalistic, autocratic culture in which he grew up. His belief about psychosis was not based on personal clinical experience but borrowed from his colleague Bleuler, who worked with schizophrenic persons in hospital and mistakenly understood dementia praecox to be a progressive neurological dementia resulting from an organic defect (Bleuler, 1911). Freud assumed that psychoses were "narcissistic neuroses" whose sufferers were unable to form a relationship (transference) to an analyst. Many analysts since have demonstrated that this is not true, and yet the accepted model of psychosis has not evolved to incorporate knowledge of Freud's and Bleuler's mistake. My own extensive clinical experience (1993, 2019) is that the structural concepts of integration and differentiation, derived from the work of psychologist Heinz Werner, enable incorporation of the psychoses into a comprehensive theory of psychopathology by situating their origin and development to failure in the phase of attachment and separation. At that critical infantile developmental juncture, function is governed by the primordial structure, and there is insufficient self-cohesion to experience intrapsychic conflict and insufficient differentiation from others to be able to reflect on one's separate self and appreciate the separateness of the other. The concepts of integration and differentiation provide a developmental explanation of the gradual transition from social predominance of the primordial structure to the secondary structure that enables "normal" and neurotic functioning, during transit of the attachment-separation phase. When pathology of development makes that transition impossible, the result is the spectrum of psychoses, characterized by absence of integration, differentiation, and formation of a cohesive self and the awareness of a separate reality of others "out there."

As homo sapiens developed the capacity for a second mental structure over the course of evolution, a fundamental change in human social organization took place from one common to other animals, that is socio-centric, and in which members are parts whose function is to sustain and equilibrate

Mental structures and the evolution of homo sapiens **101**

the system; to one based on development of individual selves, and valuation of the needs and actualization of each separate individual self. The manifestations of the complexity of mind and human behavior and accomplishment consequent to the two mental structures and their interplay include the accomplishments we call culture and civilization, and the unique depth and virulence of human destructiveness. These manifestations are the subject of a companion volume (Robbins, in press).

Humans are able to remember and record personal and cultural history, and to imagine a future that might be different; a fate over which we have some power and control because we are able to recognize forks in the road and make choices. We are not bound to our habits and to immediate reflexive responses to opportunities and changes in our environment as are members of other species whose capacity to learn is limited and who are shackled by biology for their entire lives. This evolutionary development has made humans much more concerned with self-interest and well-being, and less willing to be sacrificed as faceless parts of a larger social entity; and has led to the creation of "civilization" and all its complexities, many of which are explored in my companion volume.

This evolutionary development has led to awareness of possibilities for self-actualization beyond immediate survival and faceless sacrifice as parts of a larger social entity, and has led to the creation of civilization and all its complexities, many of which are explored in my companion volume.

For one thing, the individual maturation process responsible for the transit from the primordial structure to predominant adaptive use of the second mental structure is not always complete, because its fate is at the mercy of the vicissitudes of transit through the attachment-separation phase of development. As a result of incomplete maturation and inappropriate persistence of the primordial structure many adults are destructive to themselves, and many come into conflict with constructive elements of the broader social fabric. As we are not limited to a biologically programmed mental structure that focuses on maintaining the health of our social groupings, we find many ways to harm ourselves and our offspring, and to create social groupings that are inherently destructive or are in conflict with other social groupings.

The evolutionary development that makes humans unique may seem positive to those who do not look beyond individual human rights and values and the human achievements of civilization and culture. Such a perspective is relatively recent in human history, however, and absent in other species. How we understand the change depends on perspective and context. The gradual replacement of social groupings consistent with available resources, by groups centered around the beliefs and desires of leaders and their followers, is leading to a conflict between individual life and well-being and species survival. What seems like a solution in one context, from one perspective, seems like a problem of species survival from another.

102 Mental structures and the evolution of homo sapiens

The world population was stable until the industrial revolution, 500 years ago, and then it began to grow slowly. In 1500, it was estimated to be 461 million. 400 years later, by 1900, the advent of the technological revolution, it had grown three-fold, to about 1.6 billion. There has been an explosive five-fold growth of the population in the century and a quarter since 1900; the individual life span has tripled as well. The immediate reason, which is itself symptomatic of the deeper evolutionary change, is that technology, one of humankind's most creative achievements, has functioned to save and enhance human life and to foster creation of social structures centered around individual life and entitlement. Technology in the form of medicine and public health has functioned to save infants and children who would otherwise have died, to treat disease, and to enhance and prolong life. These developments have fueled an expansion of the population in ways that threaten the resources of the planet, the survival of other species, and produce more social conflict between humans over increasingly scarce resources and competing interests.

To understand this complexity it is necessary to consider the adequacy of the hitherto accepted exclusively biological theory of evolution, and to consider that the origin and destiny of our species might not be the same as that of others.

Even though without the unique human biology of neoteny the human difference would not have come about, biology alone is insufficient to account for it. The second mental structure, reflective thought, requires and enables acquisition of knowledge from caregivers during the lengthy period of immature dependency. This knowledge, in turn, is transmitted from one generation to another and accumulated. This knowledge serves as an independent evolutionary causal force.

There are three implications for the theory of evolution of the human difference. The first seems indisputable; complex learning and the acquisition and transmission of knowledge can serve as an independent evolutionary force, beyond biology. The second and third are mutually contradictory and we are left to take our choice or have future generations observe it firsthand. One is that the human difference is the result of an evolutionary flaw, a fatal mutation that will doom our species to extinction. A second is that homo sapiens does conform to the principles of social organization articulated by E. O. Wilson in the model articulated in his first, most influential sociobiological treatise. If that is the case, then the principle he called R, in which individual life is often sacrificed to stabilize and equilibrate the social organization, applies to human destructiveness, despite its seeming depth and virulence, as well. Were that the case, however horrifying the extent and virulence of human destructiveness may seem, it is serving the purpose of social stabilization and species preservation, and we would need to reconsider the self-centered

Mental structures and the evolution of homo sapiens **103**

beliefs and values that lead us to take extraordinary measures to preserve and enhance every human life that are defeating its purpose.

These are interesting and critical alternatives. The first will happen no matter what we do to try to stop it. The second might possibly be under human control. While the jury is not in, evidence suggests that – far from our smug belief that we humans represent the pinnacle of species evolution – the human difference and the fact of a second mental structure confront us with vexing problems related to destruction that are not encountered in other species, not only the remarkable destructiveness we seem unable to control, but the possibility of a future we do not wish to contemplate (our extinction).

To sum up, these pages have focused on the unique structuring of the human mind. Our survey has concluded that the theory of evolution needs to be re-examined and the role of psychoanalysis needs to be expanded. Psychoanalysis a critically important role both in understanding the similarities and differences between humans and other species, and in potential for understanding ourselves, our social organization, and the long-term fate of our species that might afford us more control of our destiny. A second book, *The Human Difference: Evolution, Civilization – and Destruction,* explores the major manifestations of human uniqueness and explores these questions in detail.

REFERENCES

Ainsworth, M. (1982). Attachment: Retrospect and prospect. In: C. Parkes & J. Stevenson-Hinde (Eds.), *The Place of Attachment in Human Behavior*. New York: Basic Books, pp. 3–30.

Ainsworth, M., Blehar, M., Waters, E., & Wall, S. (1978). *Patterns of Attachment: A Psychological Study of the Strange Situation*. Hillsdale, NJ: Erlbaum.

Arlow, J. & Brenner, C. (1964). *Psychoanalytic Concepts and the Structural Theory*. New York: International Universities Press.

Bastos, P., Horvath, K., Webb, J., et al. (2021). *Scientific Reports*, 11. www.doi.org/10.1038/s41598-021-97086-w

Bednarik, R. (2011). *The Human Condition*. New York: Springer.

Bell, D. (2022). Psychoanalytic reflections on the conditions of possibility of human destructiveness. *International Journal of Psycho-Analysis*, 103: 674–691.

Bion, W. (1951). *Experiences in Groups*. New York: Basic Books.

Blair, G. (2015). *The Trumps: Three Generations of Builders and a Presidential Candidate*. New York: Simon & Schuster.

Bleuler, E. (1911). *Textbook of Psychiatry*. New York: MacMillan (1924).

Boas, F. (1911). *The Mind of Primitive Man*. New York: The MacMillan Company (1938); London: Andesite Press (2017).

Bogin, B. (1997). Evolutionary hypotheses for human childhood. *Yearbook of Physical Anthropology*, 40: 63–89.

Boston Change Process Study Group (BCPSG) (2007). The foundational level of psychodynamic meaning: Implicit process in relation to conflict, defense and the dynamic unconscious. *International Journal of Psychoanalysis*, 88: 843–860.

Bowlby, J. (1969). *Attachment and Loss, Vol. I: Attachment*. London: Hogarth Press and the Institute of Psycho-Analysis.

Bowlby, J. (1973). *Attachment & Loss: VII: Separation and Anger*. New York: Basic Books.

Brucks, D., & von Bayern, A. (2020). Parrots voluntarily help each other to obtain food rewards. *Current Biology*, 30: 292–297.

Bucci, W. (1997). Discourse patterns in "good" and troubled hours: A multiple code interpretation. *Journal of the American Psychoanalytic Association*, 45: 155–187.

106 References

Bucci, W. (2000). Pathways of emotional communication. *Psychoanalytic Inquiry*, 21: 40–70.

Bucci, W. (2011). The interplay of subsymbolic and symbolic processes in psychoanalytic treatment: It takes two to tango – but who knows the steps, who's the leader? The choreography of the psychoanalytic interchange. *Psychoanalytic Dialogues*, 21: 45–54.

Capellini, I., Preston, B., McNamara, P., Barton, R, & Nunn. (2010). *Evolution of Sleep: Phylogenetic and Functional Perspectives*. London: Cambridge University Press.

Choi, J., Cutler, A., & Broersma, M. (2017). Early development of abstract language knowledge: Evidence from perception-production transfer of birth-language memory. *Royal Society Open Science*, 4: 160–166.

Chomsky, N. (1959). Review of B. F. Skinner's Verbal Behavior. *Language*, 35: 26–58.

Chomsky, N. (1965). *Aspects of the Theory of Syntax*. Cambridge, MA: MIT Press.

Chomsky, N. (1978). *Syntactic Structures*. Berlin: Mouton.

Collins, D. (1976). *The Human Evolution: From Ape to Artist*. New York & London: Penguin/Random House.

Cosans, C. (2009). *Owen's Ape & Darwin's Bulldog: Beyond Darwinism and Creationism*. Bloomington: Indiana University Press.

Darwin, C. (1859). *On the Origin of Species*. London: John Murray.

Darwin, C. (1871). *The Descent of Man, and Selection in Relation to Sex*. London: Forgotten Books, 2015.

Dawkins, R. (1976). *The Selfish Gene*. Oxford: Oxford University Press.

De Waal, F. (2016). *Are We Smart Enough to Know How Smart Animals Are?* New York: W. W. Norton.

De Waal, F. (2019). *Mama's Last Hug. Animal Emotions and What They Tell Us about Ourselves*. New York: W.W. Norton.

Descartes, R. (1637). *Discourse on the Method and Meditations on First Philosophy*. Cress, D. (Trans.). 4th Ed., 1999. Cambridge: Hackett.

Dobzhansky, T. (1937). *Genetics and the Origin of Species*. Columbia University Biological Series, V. 11. New York: Columbia University Press.

Durkin, K., Rutter, D., & Tucker, H. (1982). Social interaction and language acquisition: Motherese help you. *First Language*, 3: 107–120.

Edgerton, R. (1992). *Sick Societies*. New York: Free Press.

Eliade, M. (1964). *Shamanism: Archaic Techniques of Ecstasy*. New York: Pantheon Books.

Emde, R. (1993). Epilogue: A beginning – research approaches and expanding horizons for psychoanalysis. *Journal of the American Psychoanalytic Association*, 41S: 411–424.

Everett, D. (2005). Cultural constraints on grammar and cognition in Pirahã: Another look at the design features of human language. *Current Anthropology*, 46: 621–646.

Everett, D. (2008). *Don't Sleep, There Are Snakes: Life and Language in the Amazon Jungle*. New York: Pantheon Books.

Ferguson, C. (1964). Baby talk in six languages. *American Anthropologist*, 66: 103–114.

Fernald, A., & Kuhl, P. (1987). Acoustic determinants of infant preference for motherese speech. *Infant Behavior & Development*, 10: 279–293.

Fernald, A., & Simon, T. (1984). Expanded intonation contours in mothers' speech to newborns. *Developmental Psychology*, 20:104–113.

Freud, S. (1900). *The Interpretation of Dreams. S. E.*, 4–5. London: Hogarth Press.

Freud, S. (1909). Notes Upon a Case of Obsessional Neurosis. *S.E.* 10. London: Hogarth Press.

Freud, S. (1911). *Formulations on the Two Principles of Mental Functioning. S. E.*, 12. London: Hogarth Press.

Freud, S. (1914). *Thoughts in Times of War and Death. S. E.*, 14: 273–300. London: Hogarth Press.

Freud, S. (1915). *The Unconscious. S. E.*, 14: 166–215. London: Hogarth Press.

Freud, S. (1920). *Beyond the Pleasure Principle. S. E. 18:* 3–68. London: Hogarth Press.

Freud, S. (1930). *Civilization and Its Discontents. S. E.* 21: 59–148. London: Hogarth Press.

Freud, S. (1940). *An Outline of Psycho-Analysis. S.E.* 23: 141–208. London: Hogarth Press.

Freud, S., & Bullitt, W. (1967). *Thomas Woodrow Wilson: A Psychological Study.* New York: Houghton-Mifflin.

Freud, S., & Einstein, A. (1933). *Why War? S.E.,* 22: 197–210. London: Hogarth Press.

Gallup, G. (1970). Chimpanzees: Self-recognition. *Science,* 67: 86–87.

Gallup, G. (1977). Self recognition in primates: A comparative approach to the bidirectional properties of consciousness. *American Psychologist,* 32: 329–338.

Gallup, G. (1982). Self-Awareness and the emergence of mind in primates. *Journal of Primatology,* 2: 237–248.

Gardner, R.A., & Gardner, B. (1998). *The Structure of Learning from Sign Stimuli to Sign Language.* Hillsdale, NJ: Lawrence Erlbaum Associates.

Gardner, R.A., Gardner, B., & Van Cantfort, T. (1989). *Teaching Sign Language to Chimpanzees.* New York: SUNY Press.

Gintis, H. (2011). Gene-culture evolution and the nature of human sociality. *Philosophical Transactions B of the Royal London Biological Society*, 366: 878–888.

Goodall, J. (1986). *The Chimpanzees of Gombe: Patterns of Behavior.* New York: Belknap Press.

Goodall, J., & Berman, P. (1999). *Reason for Hope: A Spiritual Journey.* New York: Grand Central Publishing.

Goodall, J., & Wrangham, R. (2010). *In the Shadow of Man.* Boston, MA: Mariner Books.

Gould, S.J. (1977). *Ontogeny and Phylogeny.* Cambridge, MA: Harvard University Press.

Graeber, D., & Wengrow, D. (2021). *The Dawn of Everything: A New Theory of Humanity.* New York: Farrar, Straus & Giroux.

Grieser, D., & Kuhl, P. (1988). Maternal speech to infants in a tonal language: Support for universal prosodic features in motherese. *Developmental Psychology,* 24: 14–20.

Harari, Y.N. (2011). *Sapiens: A Brief History of Humankind.* New York: Harper.

Henrich, J. (2015). *The Secret of Our Success: How Culture Is Driving Human Evolution, Domesticating Our Species, and Making Us Smarter.* Princeton, NJ: Princeton University Press.

Hayes, C., & Hull, D. (Eds.) (2001). *Selection Theory and Social Construction: The Evolutionary Naturalistic Epistemology of Donald T. Campbell.* (SUNY series in Philosophy and Biology). New York: Suny Press.

Hoffman, L. (2003). Mother's ambivalence with their babies and toddlers: Manifestations of conflicts with aggression. *Journal of the American Psychoanalytic Association*, 51: 1219–1240.

Ilitis, H. (1924) *Life of Mendel.* E. & C. Paul (Trans.). New York: Norton (1932).

108 References

Isaacs, S. (1948). The nature and function of phantasy. *International Journal of Psychoanalysis*, 29: 73–97.

Jaynes, J. (1976). *The Origin of Consciousness in the Breakdown of the Bicameral Mind*. New York: Houghton Mifflin.

Jung, C.G. (1912). Two kinds of thinking. In: *Symbols of Transformation*. Bollingen Series XX V. 5, F.R.C. Hull (Trans.). New York. *The Basic Writings of C. G. Jung*. V. De Laszlo (Ed.). New York: The Modern Library (1959), pp. 10–36.

Jung, C. (Ed.) (1968). *Man and His Symbols*. New York: Dell.

Jung, C.G. (1981). The archetypes and the collective unconscious. In: *Collected Works of C.G. Jung*, Vol. 9, Part I. Princeton, NJ: Princeton University Press.

Kahneman, D. (2011). Thinking *Fast and Slow*. New York: Farrar, Straus & Giroux.

Kant, I. (1781). *Critique of Pure Reason*. W. S. Pluhar (Trans). Indianapolis/Cambridge: Hackett Publishing Company, 1996.

Kant, I. (1784). An Answer to the Question: What is Enlightenment? In: *Perpetual Peace, and other essays on politics, history, and moral practice*. T. Humphrey (Trans). Indianapolis/Cambridge: Hackett Publishing Company, 1983.

Kant, I. (1798). *Anthropology from a Pragmatic Point of View*. R. B. Louden (Trans). New York/Cambridge: Cambridge University Press, 2006.

Klein, M. (1928). Early stages of the Oedipus Complex. *International Journal of Psychoanalysis*, 9: 167–180.

Klein, M. (1946). Notes on some schizoid mechanisms. In: M. Klein (Ed.), *Envy and Gratitude and Other Works, 1946–1963*. London: Hogarth Press, pp. 1–24.

Kolata, G. (1984). Studying learning in the womb. *Science*, 225: 302–303.

Kolbert, E. (2014). *The Sixth Extinction*. New York: Henry Holt.

Kolbert, E. (2021). *Under a White Sky*. New York: Crown.

Lamarck, J. (1809). *Philosophie Zoologique, ou exposition des considérations relatives à l'histoire naturelle des animaux*. Paris: Musee de Histoire Naturelle.

Lathem, E. (Ed.) (1969). *The Poetry of Robert Frost*. New York: Holt, Rinehart & Winston.

Levy-Bruhl, L. (1923). *Primitive Mentality*. New York: AMS Press (1978).

Levy-Bruhl, L. (1928). *The Soul of the Primitive*. New York: Routledge (2016).

Levy-Bruhl, L. (1935). *Primitive Mythology*. Brisbane: University of Queensland Press, 1983.

Linnaeus, C. (1735). *Systema Naturae*. Netherlands.

Lyons-Ruth, K. (1999). The two-person unconscious: Intersubjective dialogue, enactive relational representation, and the emergence of new forms of relational organization. *Psychoanalytic Inquiry*, 19: 576–617.

Lyons-Ruth, K. (2003). Dissociation and the parent-infant dialogue. *Journal of the American Psychoanalytic Association*, 51: 883–911.

Mahler, M. (1968). *On Human Symbiosis and the Vicissitudes of Individuation: V.I: Infantile Psychosis*. New York: International Universities Press.

Mahler, M., Bergman, A., & Pine, F. (1975). *The Psychological Birth of the Human Infant: Symbiosis and Individuation*. New York: Basic Books.

Main, M. (1977). The ultimate causation of some infant attachment phenomena. *Behavioral and Brain Science*, 2: 640–643.

Main, M. (2000). The organized categories of infant, child, and adult attachment: Flexible vs. inflexible attention under attachment-related stress. *Journal of the American Psychoanalytic Association*, 48(4): 1055–1096.

Masataka, N. (1996). Perception of motherese in a signed language by 6-month-old deaf infants. *Developmental Psychology*, 32(5): 874–879.

References 109

Matte-Blanco, I. (1975). *The Unconscious as Infinite Sets: An Essay in Bi-logic*. London: Duckworth.

Matte-Blanco, I. (1988). *Thinking, Feeling, and Being: Clinical Reflections on the Fundamental Antinomy of Human Beings and World*. London: New Library of Psycho-Analysis.

May, R., Lawton, J., & Stork, N. (1995) Assessing extinction rates. In: J. Lawton, & R. May (Eds.), *Extinction Rates*. Oxford: Oxford University Press, pp. 1–24.

Mayr, E. (1963). *Animal Species and Evolution*. Cambridge, MA: Belknap Press.

Mendel, G. (1866). *Experiments on Plant Hybridization*. Lulu.com (2018).

Mesoudi, A., & Thornton, A. (2018). What is cumulative cultural evolution? *Proceedings of the Royal Society of Biological Science*. https://royalsocietypublishing.org/doi/10.1098/rspb.2018.0712.

Morel, B. (1860). *Etudes Cliniques, V.II: Traité des maladies mentales*. Paris: J.B. Bailliere.

Nicholson, S., Ed. (1987). *Shamanism*. Wheaton, IL: The Theosophical Publishing House.

Novacek, M., & Wheeler, Q. (1992). *Extinction and Phylogeny*. New York: Columbia.

Owen, R. (1860). Darwin on the origin of species. *Edinburgh Review*, 3: 487–532.

Partanen, E., Kujala, F., Naatanin, R., Lutola, A., Sambeth, A., & Huotilainen, N. (2013). Learning induced neuroplasticity in speech before birth. *Proceedings of the American Academy of Sciences,* 110: 15145–15150.

Partanen, E., & Virtala, P. (2017). Prenatal sensory development. In B. Hopkins, E. Geangu, & S. Linkenauger (Eds.), *The Cambridge Encyclopedia of Child Development*. Cambridge: Cambridge University Press, pp. 231–241.

Patterson, F. (1980). In search of man: Experiments in primate communication. *Michigan Quarterly Review, 19*: 1–15.

Paul, R. (2015). *Mixed Messages; Cultural and Genetic Inheritance in the Constitution of Human Society*. Chicago, IL: University of Chicago Press.

Paus, T., Zijdembos, A., Worsele, K., Collins, L., Blumenthal, J., Geidd, J., Rapoport, J., Evans A., et al. (1999). Structural maturation of neural pathways in children and adolescents: In vivo study. *Science*, 283: 1908–1911.

Piaget, J. (1936). *The Origins of Intelligence in Children*. New York: International Universities Press, 1952.

Pinker, S. (1994). *The Language Instinct: How the Mind Creates Language*. New York: William Morrow & Co.

Pinker, S. (2018). *Enlightenment Now: The Case for Reason, Science, Humanism and Progress*. New York: Viking.

Richerson, P., & Boyd, R. (2006). *Not by Genes Alone: How Culture Transformed Human Evolution*. Chicago, IL: University of Chicago Press.

Robbins, M. (2011). *The Primordial Mind in Health and Illness: A Cross- Cultural Perspective*. London & New York: Routledge.

Robbins, M. (2015). The "royal road" – to what? *The Annual of Psychoanalysis,* 38: 196–214.

Robbins, M. (2018a). The primary process: Freud's profound yet neglected contribution to the psychology of consciousness. *Psychoanalytic Inquiry,* 38: 186–197.

Robbins, M. (2018b). *Consciousness, Language and Self: Psychoanalytic, Linguistic and Anthropological Explorations of the Dual Nature of Mind*. London & New York: Routledge.

Robbins, M. (2019). *Psychoanalysis Meets Psychosis: Attachment, Separation, and the Undifferentiated Unintegrated Mind*. London & New York: Routledge.

Robbins, M. (in press). *The Human Difference: Evolution, Civilization – and Destruction*. London & New York: Routledge.

110 References

Robertson, J., & Robertson, J. (1971). Young children in brief separation – A fresh look. *Psychoanalytic Study of the Child*, 26: 264–315.

Savage-Rumbaugh, S. (2001). *Apes, Language and the Human Mind*. London: Oxford University Press.

Schwab, K., Groh, T., Schwab, M., & Witte, H. (2009). Nonlinear analysis and modeling of cortical activation and deactivation patterns in the immature fetal electrocorticogram. *Chaos: An Interdisciplinary Journal of Nonlinear Science*, 19(1): 015111.

Schweder, R. (2009). Has Piaget been upstaged? A reply to Hallpike. *American Anthropologist*, 87: 138–144.

Segal, H. (1993). On the clinical usefulness of the concept of death instinct. *The International Journal of Psychoanalysis*, 74: 55–61.

Selye, H. (1946). *The Stress of Life*. New York: McGraw-Hill.

Shakespeare, W. (2005). Julius Caesar Act I, Scene III, 140–141. In: S. Wells et al (Eds.), *The Oxford Shakespeare*. London: Oxford University Press.

Sharpless, E. (1985). Identity formation as reflected in the acquisition of personal pronouns. *Journal of the American Psychoanalytic Association*, 71: 861–885.

Simon, B. (1978). *Mind and Madness in Ancient Greece: The Classical Roots of Modern Psychiatry*. Ithaca, NY: Cornell University Press.

Snell, B. (1982). *The Discovery of the Mind*. (Franklin Classic) Trade Press.

Sophocles. (2000). *The Three Theban Plays*. R. Fagles (trans.). New York: Penguin Classics.

Stern, D., Sander, L., Nahum, J., Harrison, A., Lyons-Ruth, K., Morgan, A., Bruschweilerstern, N., & Tronick, E. (1998). Non-interpretive mechanisms in psychoanalytic therapy: The "something more" than interpretation. *International Journal of Psychoanalysis*, 79: 903–921.

Terrace, H. (1979). *Nim*. New York: Knopf.

Terrace, H. (2019). *Why Chimpanzees Can't Learn Language and Only Humans Can*. New York: Columbia University Press.

Trevarthen, C. (1980). The foundations of intersubjectivity: Development of interpersonal and cooperative understanding in infants. In: *The Social Foundation of Language and Thought*. D. Olson (Ed). New York: W. W. Norton, pp. 316–342.

Trevarthen, C. (2005). First things first: Infants make good use of the sympathetic rhythm of imitation, without reason or language. *Journal of Child Psychotherapy*, 31: 91–113.

Trump, M. (2020). *Too Much and Not Enough*. New York: Simon & Schuster.

van den Dungen, W. (2019). *Ancient Egyptian Writings*. Lulu.com (self-published).

Vico, G. (1744). *Principi Scienza Nuova*. Naples: Stamperia Muziana.

Werker, J. & Tees, R. (1984). Cross-language speech perception: evidence for perceptual reorganization during the first year of life. *Infant Behavior and Development*; 7: 49–63.

Werner, H. (1940). *Comparative Psychology of Mental Development*. New York: International Universities Press.

Wilson, E.O. (1975). *Sociobiology: A New Synthesis*. Cambridge, MA: Harvard University Press/Belknap Press.

Wilson, E.O. (2012). *The Social Conquest of Earth*. London: Liveright Publishing.

Winnicott, D.W. (1949). Hate in the countertransference. *International Journal of Psycho-Analysis*, 30: 69–74.

Winnicott, D.W. (1951). Transitional objects and transitional phenomena. In: *Collected Papers*. London: Tavistock, 1958, pp. 229–242.

INDEX

ACLU 94
adaptation 11, 23, 24
affect-driven categories of attachment, Ainsworth's model 41
Ainsworth, M. 41; models of attachment 42
ambivalent-resistant infants, Ainsworth's attachment theory 42
Ammaniti, M. 35
anal eroticism 76
animal intelligence 8
animistic thinking 64, 71
anxious-avoidant infants, Ainsworth's attachment theory 42
Arlow, J.: *Psychoanalytic Concepts and the Structural Theory* 3
asymmetric and symmetric logic, Matte-Blanco's model of mental function 18–19
attachment: ambivalent-resistant 42; anxious-avoidant 42, 44; attentive 42; communication 35; disorganized-disoriented 42; infant behavior 41–42; secure and insecure 39, 41, 42; theory 19
attachment-separation phase 6, 35, 43, 44, 54, 95; homo sapiens 99–101; human infants 91; maturational process 74
attentive attachment see attachment

auditory system 34; genesis and development of 35
autocratic culture 100
automatisms, behavioral 20

baby talk 36, 39; *see also* motherese; primordial mentation
Baldwin, J. 50
Bastos, A. 8
behavioral automatisms 20
belief systems 12, 21, 33, 92, 94; concrete undifferentiated 64; Lamarck's 47; obsessional 76; with reflective thought 38; sadomasochistic 76; sociobiological 51; undifferentiated omnipotent 77
bicameralism 21–22
bicameral mind hypothesis of Jaynes 22
biological theory of evolution 50; civilization and culture 51; human destructiveness 50, 53; limitation of 46–49; revision 50–54; sixth mass extinction 52; social Darwinism 52
Bion, W. 57
Blair, G. 43; *see also* Trump, D., former President, an example of primordial mental process
Bleuler, E. 100
bonobos 8, 9, 21, 49; *see also* homo sapiens; primates

112 Index

Boston Change Process Study Group
(BCPSG) 19, 42
Bowlby, J. 35, 41, 74; *see also*
attachment, theory
Boyd, R. 50
Branch Davidian cult 92
Brenner, C.: *Psychoanalytic Concepts
and the Structural Theory* 3
Bryan, W.J. 94; *see also* Scopes Monkey
Trial
Bucci, W. 20; *see also* subsymbolic
mental process

Campbell, D. 46, 50
caregivers: dependency on 34;
functional dependence on 39;
immature dependency 102;
infants of 42; learning process
from 5, 14
Chimp and Human Communication
Institute (CHCI) 10
chimpanzee (chimp): brain size and
intelligence 8, 14; DNA 49;
mental structures, humans share
with 7–15; natural environmental
and social habitat 7–8;
naturalistic observation 12
Chomsky, N. 12, 22, 23, 27, 99; *see also*
linguistic theory; recursion
civilization: cultures and 5, 14, 51, 54,
64–65, 91, 101; on reflective
representational thought 57;
signs of 65
classical psychoanalytic theory 98
co-evolution theory 50
cognitive development 20
collective cultures 58
conceptual labels 19
concreteness of animal learning 10
conflict 3, 33, 50, 53, 67, 76, 77, 87–89,
91, 96, 102; intrapsychic 6, 23,
28, 73, 74, 86, 100; maturation
23, 74, 97, 101
conscious process 16–17, 19–20, 22–24,
35, 36, 40–43, 67, 73–75, 99
contemporary Western cultures 22, 58
contextual embeddedness 10
Controversial Discussions 18
Copernicus, N. 69–70
Copernican revolution 69–70
COVID-19 31–32, 45
Creationism 94
cult systems 92–93
cultural anthropology 98

culture: autocratic 100; and civilization
5, 14, 51, 54, 64–65, 91, 101;
collective 58; contemporary
Western 22, 58; evolution 50;
gene-culture coevolution theory
50; hunter-gatherer 64; Pirahã
12, 57–61, 64; self-centric 58,
62, 67; and society 71; socio-
centric tribal 58, 62; spiritual 58,
61; Sumerian 64–65

Dark Ages 68
Darrow, C. 94; *see also* Scopes Monkey
Trial
Darwin, C. 35, 46–50, 52, 70; *The
Descent of Man* 48; hypothesis of
evolution 48, 70; and Lamarck's
Philosophie Zoologique 47; *On
the Origin of Species* 48
da Vinci, L. 69, 70
Dawkins, R. 49; *The Selfish Gene* 49
death drive 4
delusions characteristic of dreaming 78
democracy 93
Descartes, R. 11, 22, 71; *Discourse on
Method* 71
The Descent of Man (Darwin) 48
development: of dictatorship 93–94;
disturbed attachment 1, 2, 15,
43, 90, 92
dictatorship 93
disciplines: other, and their contribution
to mental structure 20–23;
psychoanalysis 16–26, 72
Discourse on Method (Descartes) 71
disorganized attachment 42
disorganized-disoriented infants 42
distinctive languages: of mental structure
27–33; primordial mental
structure 28–30; reflective
representational thought 27–28
Dobzhansky, T. 49
dreaming 23–24, 28–29, 58, 78
drive theory 3
dual inheritance theory 50
dual mental structure model 18, 23
Dungen, W. van den 66

Edgerton, R.: *Sick Societies* 50
ego 2, 3, 22, 73, 74, 98
Egyptian hieroglyphs 66
embryonic sensory-perceptual-motor
apparatus 35
Emde, R. 19

Enlightenment 46, 52, 71, 72
Enlightenment Now (Pinker) 52
Epic of Gilgamesh 66, 68
epigenetics 47, 49
epigenome 47
eusocial behavior 52–53
Everett, D. 12–13, 57–61; *Don't Sleep, There Are Snakes: Life and Language in the Amazon Jungle* 57–59; linguistic theory 13, 58; Pirahã tribe 12–13, 57–61
evolution: biological theory of (*see* biological theory of evolution); co-evolution theory 50; cultural 50; cultural anthropology and 98; Darwin's hypothesis of 48, 70; Egyptian hieroglyphic signs 66; explosive expansion of 102; genetics and 47, 49, 50–52, 55, 61, 74; hominid 9; of homo sapiens 98–103; of human civilization 63; lifespan of species 102; sixth mass extinction 52; theory of mind 1, 5

Fairbairn, R. 74
fascism 93–94
fast thinking 20, 24, 29
Ferenczi, S. 74
Ferguson, C. 36
Fred, D. 44–45
Freud, S. 22, 66, 67–68; beliefs 100; discipline of psychoanalysis 72; evolution of homo sapiens 98–103; fateful decision 17; infantile sexuality 76; *The Interpretation of Dreams* 3; mental structures (*see* mental structures); metapsychology five principles 1; neurosis *vs.* psychosis 73–79; primary process (*see* primary process); Rat Man case 75–79; secondary process 3, 16–17; selective attention 78; therapeutic method 17; unconscious process 19
Frost, R. 67
functional incompetence, primordial mentation 24–25, 30

Galileo Galilei 70
Gallese, V. 35
Gallup, G. 11, 38

Gardner, B. 8
Gardner, R.A. 8
genetics and evolution 47, 49, 50–52, 55, 61, 74; gene-culture coevolution theory 50
Gintis, H. 49
Goodall, J., originator of naturalistic observation 7, 12
Gopnik, A. 12
gorilla 9–10; *see also* homo sapiens
Graeber, D. 51
Greek epics 21, 67
Greene, M.T. 95

Haeckel, E. 47
hallucinations 17, 78
hallucinatory-delusional sense of actualization 18
Harari, U.N. 52; *Sapiens* 52
Henrich, J. 50
hive-minded super-cooperators 53
hominid evolution 9
homo sapiens 5, 21, 55, 63; bonobos 8, 9, 21, 49; chimp (*see* chimpanzee (chimp)); evolution of 98–103; gorilla 9–10
Hooff, J. van 12
human difference: civilization and 5, 14, 50, 51, 54, 65, 101; destructive aspect of 51; implications for 102–103; neoteny 5, 14, 39, 47, 53, 54, 63, 65, 99, 102
The Human Difference: Evolution, Civilization – and Destruction (Robbins) 103
human infants: attachment-separation phase 91; language expressive of 30; mental activity of animals and 11–13; newborn 36; relative immaturity of 5; sensory-perceptual capacity development 13; *see also* infants
human mind 1–2, 5, 16, 20, 23, 28, 68, 98, 103
human social structure 62, 63
human species 91; *vs.* animals 56
hunter-gatherer culture 64

id 2, 3, 73, 98
identity 89, 92; human aspect 28; infant, elements of 30; sensory-perceptual 17; undifferentiated family 44
Iliad 66

114 Index

immediacy of experience principle 58
individuality 61, 68, 69, 99; maturation 101; psychopathology 33; self-actualization 96; separation and 74
industrial revolution 67, 71, 102
infantile sensory-perceptual-motor recognition of mother 19
infants: ambivalent-resistant 42; anxious-avoidant 42; attachment behavior 41–42; attachment-separation phase 91; of caregivers 42; disorganized-disoriented 42; identity elements 30; language expressive of 30; mental activity of animals and 11–13; newborn 36; relative immaturity of 5; secure 42; sensory-perceptual capacity, development of 13; *see also* human infants
insecure attachment 41
instinct theory 3–4; biological theory of evolution 46–54, 102; Freud's theory of mind 1, 5; life (Eros) and death (Thanatos) 4
instrumental language learning 9
intelligence 10; animal 8; attribute of 11; chimp 8, 14; conscious and 99; similarities and differences between homo sapiens and other species 8, 10–11, 12, 99
The Interpretation of Dreams (Freud) 3
Isaacs, S. 18
Israeli American Council 31

Jaynes, J. 20–22, 66; bicameral mind hypothesis 21–22

Kahneman, D. 20, 24, 29; *Thinking Fast and Slow* 20
Kant, I. 3, 16, 67–68, 72; tripartite mind hypothesis 3, 72
Kanzi 9
K behavior *or* kin selection 56
Kea parrot 8
kin selection *see* K behavior *or* kin selection
Klein, M. 18, 74, 77, 89; paranoid-schizoid position hypothesis 18, 89
Knox, B. 66
Kolata, G. 36

Kolbert, E. 51, 52; sixth mass extinction hypothesis 52
Koresh, D. 92

Lamarck, Chevalier de, and inheritance of acquired characteristics 47
languages: and belief 38; motherese 36; Pirahã 57–61; and primordial mental structure 28–30; and primordial mentation 3, 30, 33, 57, 81; and reflective representational thought 27–28; relationship to reflective thought 17, 22, 33, 36, 40, 99; self-awareness and 11; structural determinants of 30
LaPlanche, J. 3
learning: animal 10; from caregivers 5, 14; creative 11, 15, 41; instrumental language 9; neurological foundation of 35; relationship to reflective representational thought 5, 11, 53, 63; situational 10; survival based 52–54
lemurs 8
Levy-Bruhl, L. 20, 21
life instinct (Eros) 4
linguistic theory 12, 22, 23, 99
Linnaeus, C. 46, 48; and evolution of species 46, 48
Lyons-Ruth, K. 19, 42; strange situation experiment 41

Mahler, M. 37, 74; symbiosis concept 74
Main, M. 42; types of disturbed attachment 42–43
maladaptive functioning 75
Mama's Last Hug (de Waals) 12
Manson, C. 92
mark test, of Gordon Gallup 11
Masataka, N. 36
Matte-Blanco, I., theory of symmetric and asymmetric mind 18
maturation 34; attachment-separation phase 74; healthy 5–6; human 5, 9, 11, 12, 14; individual 101; neurobiological and psychosocial 14; primate and other species 9, 13–14, 34, 39, 56, 65, 84
mature conflict 97
mature mind 5–6, 21
Maxims of Ptahhotep (Ptahhotep) 65
Mayr, E. 49

Mendel, G., contribution to plant genetics 49
mental structures 91–97; biological theory of evolution 46–49; concept of 1–2; distinctive languages of 27–33; and healthy maturation 5–6; history in psychoanalysis and other disciplines 16–26; homo sapiens 98–103; humans share with other primates 7–15; nature of 1–4; neural structures and 3–4; from other disciplines 20–23; from psychoanalysis and other disciplines 16–26; during separation phase of development 39–45; social structure 55–62; *see also* second mental structure
mentation: mental development unique to humans 16, 74; of other animal species 20; primordial (*see* primordial mentation); and reflective representational thought 5, 23; unconscious 16
metapsychology, Freud's five principles 1
mirror test of Gordon Gallup 11, 38
molecular genetics 49
motherese, nature of: by infant researchers 25; mutation/flawed evolution 102; in sign language 36
mythopoesis 21

narcissistic neuroses 100
narratization 22
naturalistic observation, Jane Goodall 7–6, 12
natural selection, Darwin's hypothesis of 47–49
nature-nurture debate 17, 35
neoteny 5, 14, 39, 47, 49, 53, 63, 65, 99, 102
neural structures 3–4
neuro-psychoanalysis discipline 4
neuroscience and nature-nurture controversy 35; as offshoot of technology 35
neurosis 6, 73–90
A New Synthesis (Wilson) 55
Newton, I. 70
non-animal species 7
nonconscious mental activity 19

Oedipus tale 67
omnipotence 37, 77–78
On the Origin of Species (Darwin) 48
Owens, B. 48

parallel evolution of reflective thought and self-centered social organization 63–72
paranoid-schizoid position, of Klein 18
Partanen, E. 36
pathological development 6
Patterson, F. 8, 9
Phaedrus (Plato) 2
phantasy 18; distinct from fantasy 77; *see also* Klein, M., paranoid-schizoid position hypothesis
phenotypes 49–51; and genotypes 47
Philosophie Zoologique (Lamarck) 47
Piaget, J. 20, 66; Piaget's stage model 20, 24, 30
Pinker, S. 12, 28, 52; *Enlightenment Now* 52
Pirahã culture 12, 57–61, 64
Plato, tripartite model of mind 2, 16; logistikon (thought or reason) 3
Pontalis, J. 3
population: explosive growth 53; five-fold growth of 102; genetics 49; regulation by R & K 55–56; science spawned technology 71; unique proliferation of 22
pre-Oedipal phase 73
primary process, of Freud 2–3, 16, 28, 74; discovery of 20–22; feature of 17; immature function 17–18; intelligence from 99; problems with concept of 1, 4, 20–22
primates 3, 34, 38, 39, 46, 54–56, 62, 65; research 7–15
primatology 12; primordial mind 4, 21; R and K behaviors 55–56
primordial mental structure 10, 21–22, 24, 66; characteristics of 23–24; common to many species 34–38; concept of 16; derivatives of 17; languages and 28–30; neurosis *vs.* psychosis 73–90; to reflective thought 69; social organization 55–62
primordial mentation 24–26, 28, 40, 93; chimp and bonobo researchers 8; contradiction characteristic of 83; and fantasy play 41; fast thinking 20, 24, 29; language and 3, 30,

116 Index

33, 57, 81; and reflective thought 38, 75; representatives of 96; simplistic belief 29; social world of 71

Psychoanalytic Concepts and the Structural Theory (Arlow and Brenner) 3

psychopathology 73; Freud's model of 100; individual 33

psychosis 6, 73–90, 94, 100

Ptahhotep: *Maxims of Ptahhotep* 65

Ptolemaic cosmology 70

quasi-religious, of Richard Owen: definition of species 48; movement 1

Rank, O. 74

Rat Man, Freud's case of obsessional neurosis 75–79

R behaviors 55–56

realistic conflict theory of Donald Campbell 50

recursion 12, 28, 30; in Chomsky's theory of language 23, 27

reflective representational thought 3, 11–12, 20, 22, 63; civilizations based on 57; languages structure 27–28; self-reference and 39; separate and distinct in 66; structure 23

relational theory 19

religious beliefs 49; long-standing 7; passionate 25

religious extremism 93

REM sleep 34

Renaissance 69

Richerson, P. 50

Robertson, J. 35

sadomasochistic belief system 76

Safina, C. 12

Sapiens (Harari) 52

Savage-Rumbaugh, S. 8, 9

schizophrenia 75, 79, 82, 86

Scholasticism 69

Schweder, R. 24, 30

science and technology 21, 58; as civilized progress 69, 71

scientific theory of evolution 47, 94

Scopes, J.T. *see* Scopes Monkey Trial

Scopes Monkey Trial 92, 94

secondary process 16–17

second mental structure 99; biological theory of evolution 46–49; parallel evolution of 63–72; self-centric culture based on 67; during separation phase of development 39–45; and social changes 101; *see also* mental structures

secure attachment 39, 41, 42, 91

Segal, H. 18

self-awareness 8, 40; animal development of 11; reflective 11–12, 74

self-centric cultures 58, 62, 67

self-centric social organization 63–72

selfhood 68, 69

The Selfish Gene (Dawkins) 49

self-reference 39

self-reflection 73

self-satisfaction 68

sense of self, objectification and self-awareness 11

sensory-motor stage of Piaget 5

sensory-perceptual identity 17

separation-individuation 74

separation process: attachment-separation phase (*see* attachment-separation phase); mental structures during 39–45

shared social-cultural knowledge 53

Sick Societies (Edgerton) 50

sign language 9, 10, 36

signs and symbols 51

Simon, B., model of ancient Greek mentation 66

situational learning 10

sixth mass extinction, hypothesis of Kolbert 52

Smithsonian Human Evolution Project 49

Snell, B. 66

social awareness 93

social conflict 53, 96–97, 102

The Social Conquest of Earth (Wilson) 52

social-cultural knowledge 53

social destructiveness 91–97

social organization 8, 91–97; complex forms of 51; primordial mental structures 55–62; reflection about human 52; self-centric 63–72

social structure 55–63

social systems 25, 33, 55, 68, 92

society 92, 98; classes of 3; culture and 71; human 52, 55

Index **117**

Sociobiology, theory of E.O. Wilson 55
socio-centric social organization 63–72
socio-centric tribal cultures 58, 62
sociology 73, 98
Socrates' understanding of mind 2
somatic process 18
species, classification by Linnaeus
46–49; Darwin's theory (see
Darwin, C.); lifespan of 102;
social organization 52; see also
homo sapiens
spiritual cultures 58, 61
Stern, D. 19
strange situation experiment, of Mary
Ainsworth 41
subsymbolic mental process, of Bucci
20; non-verbal processing 20
Sumerian culture 64–65
superego 2, 3, 73, 98
survival of the fittest 56
symbolization 23, 28, 29, 58, 61, 64,
71; emotional significance 67;
mental map 59; and phonetic
linkage 64; reflective thought 20,
40, 79; somatic-motoric-sensory-
perceptual experience 19
symmetric and asymmetric logic,
Matte-Blanco's model of mental
function 18–19
systematics, theory of 46, 49

Tees, R. 37
Terrace, H. 8, 10
theory of evolution 5, 54; biological (see
biological theory of evolution);
biological reductive survival-
adaptive 54; causal importance
of human learning 4, 46; human
difference, implications for
102–103; implications for 102;
limitations of reductive biological
theory 4, 54
theory of symmetric and asymmetric
mind, by Matte-Blanco 18
Thinking Fast and Slow (Kahneman) 20
third trimester of pregnancy, changes in
fetus 34, 35

Trevarthen, C. 36
tribal culture 24–25, 28–29; and belief
57–58; dreaming 24; Pirahã tribe
12–13, 57–61; and socio-centric
mental structure 58
tripartite model of mind, Freud: dual
mental structure 18; of individual
mind 3, 72; mental structures
2–3, 18; see also
Freud, S.
Trump, D., former President, an example
of primordial mental process 26,
30–33, 43–45, 94–95

unconscious process 16–21, 24, 76, 79,
89, 99
universal grammar, language model of
Chomsky 99

violence 93, 95; and destructiveness 51;
war and 52

Waals, F. de 7, 10, 12; *Mama's Last Hug*
12
Waddington, C. 47
Wallace, A.R. 48
war: and destructiveness 51; Freud-
Einstein correspondence *Why
War?* 107; and violence 52;
World War II 18, 33
Washoe 9
Werker, J. 37
Werner, H. 5–6, 100; developmental
theory of syncretism 5;
integration and differentiation
5–6
Westboro Baptist Church 92
Western cultural beliefs 38
Wilson, E.O. 51–57, 91, 102; eusocial
52–53; *A New Synthesis* 55; R &
K regulatory principles 54, 56;
The Social Conquest of Earth 52;
social group differences between
homo sapiens and other species
52–53, 57; Sociobiology 51, 54,
55, 91, 102
Winnicott, D.W. 37, 41, 74

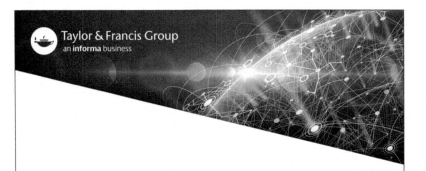